DEREK VALE

Python for Beginners

100+ Hands-on coding challenges

Copyright © 2024 by Derek Vale

All rights reserved. No part of this publication may be reproduced, stored or transmitted in any form or by any means, electronic, mechanical, photocopying, recording, scanning, or otherwise without written permission from the publisher. It is illegal to copy this book, post it to a website, or distribute it by any other means without permission.

First edition

This book was professionally typeset on Reedsy. Find out more at reedsy.com

Contents

Getting Started with Python Fundamentals	1
Control Flow Essentials	25
Functions and Problem Decomposition	57
Mastering Data Structures (Lists, Tuples, Sets,...)	95
String Manipulation and Text Processing	121
Working with Files and Basic Data Handling	157
Debugging and Optimization	197
Object-Oriented Programming Essentials	238
Advanced Topics for Beginners	286
Putting It All Together – Projects and Real-World...	330

Getting Started with Python Fundamentals

Getting Started with Python Fundamentals
Python is often celebrated as one of the most accessible programming languages for beginners, and for good reason. Its clean syntax and intuitive structure make it easy to learn while still being powerful enough for a wide range of applications, from web development to data analysis. This chapter will introduce you to the essential building blocks of Python, providing the foundation you'll need to understand more complex programming concepts later on. As you go through this chapter, you'll get familiar with the syntax and structure that make Python unique. By the end, you'll be ready to tackle your first coding challenges with confidence.

Python Basics: Syntax and Structure

Python's syntax—its rules and guidelines for writing code— is designed to be readable and straightforward. Unlike some other programming languages that use symbols and complex syntax, Python focuses on simplicity and readability, making it ideal for beginners. Here's a breakdown of Python's core syntax and structural elements that will form the basis of everything you write in Python.

1. Python Code Blocks and Indentation

In Python, indentation is crucial. Unlike many other programming languages that use braces {} to define code blocks (such as for loops, if statements, or functions), Python relies on indentation to structure code. Each level of indentation (typically four spaces or a single tab) indicates a new block. This approach not only enforces readability but also reduces the likelihood of errors due to misplaced braces or parentheses.

Example:

```python
if condition:
    # Code inside this block
    print("Condition is true")
# Code here is outside the if block
```

In this example, the print statement is part of the if-statement block because it is indented. When the indentation ends, Python understands that the if-statement block is complete.

2. Basic Syntax Rules

To write clear and effective Python code, you'll need to follow a few essential syntax rules:

- **Case Sensitivity**: Python is case-sensitive, so Variable, variable, and VARIABLE would be considered different identifiers.
- **Commenting**: Use # to write comments, which Python ignores during execution. Comments are useful for explaining your code or making notes for future reference.
- Example:

```python
# This is a comment
print("Hello, world!")  # This prints a message to the console
```

- **End of Line**: Unlike many other languages, Python does not require a semicolon ; at the end of each line. Instead, a newline signifies the end of a statement.

3. Variables and Data Types

Variables in Python allow you to store and manipulate data. Declaring a variable in Python is straightforward: simply assign a value to a variable name using the = operator.

Example:

```python
name = "Alice"
age = 25
is_student = True
```

Python is a dynamically typed language, meaning you don't need to specify the data type of a variable when declaring it. The interpreter determines the data type based on the value assigned. Python supports several built-in data types:

- **Integer (int)**: Whole numbers, such as 5 or -3.
- **Float (float)**: Numbers with a decimal point, such as 3.14 or -0.001.
- **String (str)**: Text, enclosed in quotes ("hello" or 'hello').
- **Boolean (bool)**: True or False values, typically used in conditional statements.

4. Working with Strings

Strings in Python are sequences of characters enclosed in single (' ') or double (" ") quotes. Strings are versatile and come with several built-in methods for manipulation.

Example:

```python
greeting = "Hello, World!"
print(greeting.lower())  # Outputs: "hello, world!"
print(greeting.upper())  # Outputs: "HELLO, WORLD!"
print(len(greeting))     # Outputs: 13
```

Python strings are immutable, meaning you cannot modify them directly after they are created. Instead, any string manipulation creates a new string.

5. Basic Operators

Python includes several operators to perform calculations, compare values, and work with data:

- **Arithmetic Operators**: +, -, *, /, ** (exponent), % (modulus)
- Example:

```python
result = 10 + 5
print(result)  # Outputs: 15
```

- **Comparison Operators**: ==, !=, >, <, >=, <= are used to compare values and return a boolean result.
- Example:

```python
print(10 > 5)   # Outputs: True
print(10 == 5)  # Outputs: False
```

- **Logical Operators**: and, or, not are used to combine or invert

conditions.
- Example:

```python
is_raining = True
has_umbrella = False
print(is_raining and has_umbrella)   # Outputs: False
```

These operators form the basis of Python's ability to perform calculations, make comparisons, and control the flow of a program.

6. Basic Input and Output

Python's print() function is used to display output to the console, and input() is used to gather input from users.
Example:

```python
name = input("Enter your name: ")
print("Hello, " + name + "!")
```

This program prompts the user to enter their name, then outputs a greeting. The input() function always returns data as a string, so you may need to convert it to another data type if needed.

7. Working with Conditions and Control Flow

Conditional statements allow a program to execute certain code based on specific conditions. The if statement is the foundation of control flow in Python, enabling decision-making in your code.
Example:

python

```python
age = 18
if age >= 18:
    print("You are an adult.")
else:
    print("You are a minor.")
```

This code uses an if-else structure to check if a person's age is 18 or older, printing different messages based on the result. You can expand this with elif for additional conditions.

8. Looping with for and while

Loops allow you to repeat a block of code multiple times, useful for tasks like processing data or iterating through lists. Python has two primary loop types:

- **for loop**: Used to iterate over sequences like lists or ranges.
- Example:

python

```python
for i in range(5):
    print(i)
# Outputs: 0, 1, 2, 3, 4
```

- **while loop**: Runs as long as a condition is true.
- Example:

python

```
count = 0
while count < 5:
    print(count)
    count += 1
```

Each loop type serves different purposes. for loops are great for definite iterations, while while loops are better suited for indefinite ones.

9. Defining Functions

Functions in Python allow you to bundle code into reusable pieces, making your programs more modular and organized. Use the def keyword to define a function.

Example:

python

```
def greet(name):
    print("Hello, " + name + "!")
```

To use the function, simply call it with an argument:

python

```
greet("Alice")   # Outputs: Hello, Alice!
```

Functions can take multiple parameters, return values, and even contain nested functions.

10. Error Handling Basics

Python provides error handling using try, except, and finally blocks, helping you manage and respond to errors gracefully.

Example:

```python
try:
    result = 10 / 0
except ZeroDivisionError:
    print("Cannot divide by zero.")
finally:
    print("Execution complete.")
```

Here, the except block catches a division error, while finally executes regardless of whether an error occurs.

Understanding Python's syntax and structure is essential for writing efficient, readable code. Mastering these basics will prepare you for more complex programming tasks and problem-solving challenges. As you continue, practice writing code that follows these conventions, and don't hesitate to experiment—Python is very forgiving for beginners and encourages exploration.

Challenge 1–10: Printing, Variables, and Simple Operations

This section introduces you to some fundamental aspects of programming in Python. We'll explore variable assignment, perform arithmetic operations, and manipulate strings. These concepts might seem simple, but they are essential for building the foundation of your programming skills. Each challenge here builds on the previous one, gradually introducing you to new elements in a logical progression.

Challenge 1: Hello, World!

Objective: Write a program that prints "Hello, World!" to the console.

This is a classic starting point for programming in any language. In Python, printing text to the console is straightforward with the print() function.

GETTING STARTED WITH PYTHON FUNDAMENTALS

Instructions:
1. Write a Python script that uses print() to output the phrase "Hello, World!".
2. Run the script to see your message displayed.

Solution:

```python
print("Hello, World!")
```

Explanation: The print() function is used to display information to the console. By enclosing "Hello, World!" in quotation marks, you indicate that it's a string of text.

Challenge 2: Assigning Variables

Objective: Assign values to variables and display them.

Variables are like storage boxes for data. You can assign values to them, use them in calculations, or modify them later. Python allows you to assign values to variables easily.

Instructions:

1. Create a variable named name and assign it your name as a string.
2. Create another variable called age and assign it an integer value for your age.
3. Print both variables in a complete sentence.

Solution:

```python
name = "Alice"
age = 25
```

```
print("My name is " + name + " and I am " + str(age) + " years
old.")
```

Explanation: We assigned "Alice" to name and 25 to age. Notice how we use str(age) to convert the integer age to a string so it can be concatenated with other strings in the print statement.

Challenge 3: Basic Arithmetic Operations

Objective: Perform addition, subtraction, multiplication, and division with variables.

Python allows you to do basic arithmetic operations easily. These operations include addition (+), subtraction (-), multiplication (*), and division (/).

Instructions:

1. Create two variables, x and y, with integer values.
2. Perform addition, subtraction, multiplication, and division on these variables.
3. Print the results of each operation.

Solution:

```python
x = 10
y = 3
print("Addition:", x + y)           # Outputs: 13
print("Subtraction:", x - y)        # Outputs: 7
print("Multiplication:", x * y)     # Outputs: 30
print("Division:", x / y)           # Outputs: 3.3333333333333335
```

Explanation: Each arithmetic operation is performed using standard operators. The division operator / in Python always produces a floating-point result, even if the division is exact.

GETTING STARTED WITH PYTHON FUNDAMENTALS

Challenge 4: String Concatenation

Objective: Combine multiple strings into a single string.

String concatenation lets you join multiple strings into one. This is useful when you want to create custom messages or merge pieces of data together.

Instructions:

1. Create two string variables: first_name and last_name.
2. Concatenate them with a space in between to form a full name.
3. Print the full name.

Solution:

```python
first_name = "John"
last_name = "Doe"
full_name = first_name + " " + last_name
print("Full name:", full_name)
```

Explanation: The + operator is used to concatenate first_name and last_name with a space in between. This results in a complete name, "John Doe."

Challenge 5: Using Variables in Calculations

Objective: Use variables to calculate and display the area of a rectangle.

Variables can represent numbers in calculations. Here, you'll use variables for the length and width of a rectangle, then calculate its area.

Instructions:

1. Assign values to length and width.
2. Calculate the area of the rectangle (Area = length × width).
3. Print the result.

Solution:

```python
length = 5
width = 10
area = length * width
print("The area of the rectangle is:", area)
```

Explanation: The area of a rectangle is calculated by multiplying its length by its width. The result is stored in area and printed.

Challenge 6: Calculating with Multiple Variables

Objective: Calculate the average of three numbers.

This challenge uses variables to store multiple numbers and calculates their average.

Instructions:

1. Assign values to three variables: num1, num2, and num3.
2. Calculate the average of these numbers.
3. Print the average.

Solution:

```python
num1 = 10
num2 = 20
num3 = 30
average = (num1 + num2 + num3) / 3
print("The average is:", average)
```

Explanation: Adding num1, num2, and num3 and then dividing by 3 gives the average. The result is stored in average and printed.

Challenge 7: String Formatting with Variables

GETTING STARTED WITH PYTHON FUNDAMENTALS

Objective: Use string formatting to create a sentence with variables.

Python provides various ways to insert variables into strings. String formatting allows for readable, dynamic messages.

Instructions:

1. Create variables city and temperature.
2. Print a sentence describing the temperature in the city using string formatting.

Solution:

```python
city = "New York"
temperature = 75
print(f"The temperature in {city} is {temperature} degrees Fahrenheit.")
```

Explanation: The f before the string allows us to insert variables directly into it with curly braces {}.

Challenge 8: Using the Modulus Operator

Objective: Calculate the remainder of a division using the modulus operator.

The modulus operator % returns the remainder of a division operation. This operator is useful in various applications, like checking if a number is even or odd.

Instructions:

1. Create two variables, a and b, with integer values.
2. Use the modulus operator to find the remainder when a is divided by b.
3. Print the result.

Solution:

```python
a = 10
b = 3
remainder = a % b
print("The remainder of", a, "divided by", b, "is:", remainder)
```

Explanation: Here, 10 % 3 results in 1, which is the remainder of dividing 10 by 3.

Challenge 9: Basic String Manipulation

Objective: Modify strings using built-in methods.

Python provides built-in methods to manipulate strings easily. For example, you can change the case of a string or remove white spaces.

Instructions:

1. Create a variable message with the value " Python Programming ".
2. Use string methods to:

- Convert it to uppercase.
- Remove leading and trailing spaces.

1. Print the modified string.

Solution:

```python
message = "   Python Programming   "
print("Uppercase:", message.upper())      # Outputs: "   PYTHON PROGRAMMING   "
print("Trimmed:", message.strip())        # Outputs: "Python
```

Programming"

Explanation: The upper() method converts the string to uppercase, while strip() removes any whitespace at the start and end of the string.

Challenge 10: Combining Arithmetic and Strings

Objective: Perform a calculation and print the result in a sentence.

You can combine arithmetic operations with strings to create meaningful output messages.

Instructions:

1. Create two variables, radius and pi, and assign them values.
2. Calculate the area of a circle using the formula Area = pi * radius^2.
3. Print the result as part of a complete sentence.

Solution:

```python
radius = 5
pi = 3.14159
area = pi * (radius ** 2)
print("The area of a circle with radius", radius, "is", area)
```

Explanation: We calculate the area by squaring radius and multiplying by pi. The result is included in a sentence that provides context.

By completing these challenges, you're gaining proficiency in core programming skills—variables, arithmetic, and string manipulation. These tasks may seem simple, but they're essential for understanding how to build and manage data within your programs.

Solutions and Explanations

This section provides detailed explanations and solutions for each of the challenges in **Chapter 1: Printing, Variables, and Simple Operations**.

Reviewing these explanations will help reinforce the concepts covered, ensuring you understand the logic behind each solution and how to apply these basic operations in Python.

Challenge 1 Solution and Explanation: Hello, World!
Solution:

```python
print("Hello, World!")
```

Explanation: The print() function in Python is used to output text or other information to the console. By enclosing "Hello, World!" in quotation marks, we define it as a *string*, a sequence of characters. Python will interpret anything inside the parentheses and display it, making this a quick and effective way to print a message.

Challenge 2 Solution and Explanation: Assigning Variables
Solution:

```python
name = "Alice"
age = 25
print("My name is " + name + " and I am " + str(age) + " years old.")
```

Explanation: Here, we create two variables, name and age, which store a string and an integer, respectively. In the print statement, we use string concatenation (+) to combine different pieces of information into a single output. Since age is an integer, we convert it to a string using str(age) before concatenating it with the other strings. Python requires variables in concatenations to be of the same type, so using str() here prevents errors and ensures compatibility.

Challenge 3 Solution and Explanation: Basic Arithmetic Operations

GETTING STARTED WITH PYTHON FUNDAMENTALS

Solution:

```python
x = 10
y = 3
print("Addition:", x + y)
print("Subtraction:", x - y)
print("Multiplication:", x * y)
print("Division:", x / y)
```

Explanation: This solution demonstrates Python's four basic arithmetic operators: + (addition), - (subtraction), * (multiplication), and / (division). Each operation is performed on the variables x and y. Division in Python using / always returns a float, even when the result is a whole number. If you only want the whole number part of the division, you can use // (floor division), which discards any decimal part.

Challenge 4 Solution and Explanation: String Concatenation
Solution:

```python
first_name = "John"
last_name = "Doe"
full_name = first_name + " " + last_name
print("Full name:", full_name)
```

Explanation: In this challenge, we combine two strings using the + operator, which is known as *string concatenation*. By adding a space " " between first_name and last_name, we ensure the resulting full_name has a natural separation. Concatenating strings in this way is useful for formatting text output that includes multiple pieces of information.

Challenge 5 Solution and Explanation: Using Variables in Calculations
Solution:

```python
length = 5
width = 10
area = length * width
print("The area of the rectangle is:", area)
```

Explanation: To calculate the area of a rectangle, we multiply length by width using the * operator. Storing the result in area keeps the calculation organized and allows easy reference for later use. This example demonstrates how Python can perform calculations and assign the results to variables for use in subsequent lines.

Challenge 6 Solution and Explanation: Calculating with Multiple Variables

Solution:

```python
num1 = 10
num2 = 20
num3 = 30
average = (num1 + num2 + num3) / 3
print("The average is:", average)
```

Explanation: The average is calculated by adding num1, num2, and num3 together and dividing the result by 3. By grouping the addition with parentheses, we ensure it's calculated before the division. Python's order of operations (PEMDAS: Parentheses, Exponents, Multiplication and Division, Addition and Subtraction) prioritizes operations within parentheses first, so this approach calculates the sum of all three numbers before dividing, as intended.

Challenge 7 Solution and Explanation: String Formatting with Variables

Solution:

GETTING STARTED WITH PYTHON FUNDAMENTALS

```python
city = "New York"
temperature = 75
print(f"The temperature in {city} is {temperature} degrees Fahrenheit.")
```

Explanation: Python's *f-strings* (formatted string literals) provide a simple way to insert variables directly into strings. By prefixing the string with f, you can include variable names within curly braces {}. Python replaces the braces with the variable's value, resulting in a dynamic message. F-strings offer a clean, readable way to incorporate variables into output without needing to use multiple + operators for concatenation.

Challenge 8 Solution and Explanation: Using the Modulus Operator
Solution:

```python
a = 10
b = 3
remainder = a % b
print("The remainder of", a, "divided by", b, "is:", remainder)
```

Explanation: The modulus operator % returns the remainder of dividing one number by another. In this example, 10 % 3 yields a remainder of 1, because 10 divided by 3 is 3 with a remainder of 1. This operation is helpful in many contexts, such as determining if a number is even or odd (n % 2 results in 0 for even numbers and 1 for odd).

Challenge 9 Solution and Explanation: Basic String Manipulation
Solution:

```python
message = "   Python Programming   "
print("Uppercase:", message.upper())
```

```python
print("Trimmed:", message.strip())
```

Explanation: The upper() method converts all characters in message to uppercase, making it ideal for cases where you want consistent capitalization. The strip() method removes any whitespace from the beginning and end of message, which is especially useful when processing user input that may contain unwanted spaces.

Challenge 10 Solution and Explanation: Combining Arithmetic and Strings

Solution:

```python
radius = 5
pi = 3.14159
area = pi * (radius ** 2)
print("The area of a circle with radius", radius, "is", area)
```

Explanation: This challenge demonstrates combining calculations with strings to create meaningful output. The area of a circle is calculated using the formula pi * radius^2, where ** is Python's exponent operator. The result, stored in area, is then included in a descriptive sentence using print().

Each challenge in this section introduces key aspects of Python syntax, structure, and basic operations. Mastering these fundamentals will enable you to handle more complex programming tasks, building a strong foundation for advanced coding challenges. As you progress through the book, continue applying these basic principles—they will serve as the backbone of your Python skills.

Test Your Knowledge: Quick Quiz on Python Basics

This quiz is designed to reinforce what you've learned about Python fundamentals so far. Answer the questions to test your understanding of variables, arithmetic, strings, and basic operations. Try to answer each question before checking the answers provided at the end of the quiz.

Question 1:

Which of the following statements correctly prints the text "Welcome to Python!" to the console?

a) print(Welcome to Python!)
b) print("Welcome to Python!")
c) echo "Welcome to Python!"
d) display("Welcome to Python!")

Question 2:

What will the following code output?

```python
x = 5
y = 10
print(x + y)
```

a) x + y
b) 510
c) 15
d) 5 + 10

Question 3:

Which of these is the correct way to declare a variable in Python?

a) 5num = 10
b) num-1 = 10
c) number = 10
d) int number = 10

Question 4:

What is the result of the following expression?

```python
print(7 % 2)
```

a) 3
   b) 1
   c) 0
   d) 2

Question 5:
Given the following code, what will the output be?

```python
name = "Alice"
print("Hello, " + name)
```

a) Hello, Alice
   b) Hello name
   c) Hello Alice
   d) Hello + name

Question 6:
In Python, which symbol is used for exponentiation (raising to a power)?
a) *
b) **
c) ^
d) %

Question 7:
What does the following code output?

```python
message = "   Learn Python!   "
print(message.strip())
```

a) " Learn Python! "

b) "LearnPython!"
c) "Learn Python!"
d) "Learn Python"

Question 8:

If you want to calculate the area of a rectangle with length 8 and width 5, which of these statements is correct?

a) area = length * width
b) area = 8 x 5
c) area = 8 + 5
d) area = length + width

Question 9:

What will the following code output?

```python
radius = 3
pi = 3.14159
print(pi * radius ** 2)
```

a) 28.27331
b) 9.42477
c) 3.14159
d) 18.84954

Question 10:

Which of these expressions correctly concatenates the strings "Hello" and "World" with a space in between?

a) print("Hello" + "World")
b) print("Hello", "World")
c) print("Hello " + "World")
d) print("Hello" + " World")

Answer Key

1. **b)** print("Welcome to Python!")
2. **c)** 15

3. **c)** number = 10
4. **b)** 1 (7 divided by 2 gives a remainder of 1)
5. **a)** Hello, Alice
6. **b)** ** (used for exponentiation)
7. **c)** "Learn Python!" (strip removes spaces from both ends)
8. **a)** area = length * width
9. **a)** 28.27331 (area of circle formula: pi * radius^2)
10. **d)** print("Hello" + " World") (adds a space after "Hello" for correct spacing)

Review your answers and revisit any concepts that were unclear. Practicing these basics will strengthen your foundation and prepare you for the next set of coding challenges.

Control Flow Essentials

Overview: Understanding Conditional Statements and Loops

In programming, **control flow** refers to the direction in which a program's statements are executed. Control flow structures allow you to dictate the flow of your code based on various conditions and repetitive tasks. In Python, two of the primary tools for controlling flow are **conditional statements** and **loops**.

This section covers the fundamentals of conditional statements, which enable decision-making, and loops, which allow repetitive execution of code. Mastering these concepts is crucial, as they form the backbone of logic in almost any program you'll write.

1. Conditional Statements

Conditional statements are used to run specific blocks of code based on whether a condition is true or false. Python offers several types of conditional structures:

1.1 The if Statement

The if statement is the most basic form of decision-making. It checks whether a specified condition evaluates to True. If it does, the code inside the if block is executed; otherwise, it is skipped.

Syntax:

```python
```

```
if condition:
    # Code to execute if condition is True
```

Example:

```python
age = 18
if age >= 18:
    print("You are eligible to vote.")
```

In this example, the message will only print if age is 18 or greater. If the condition age >= 18 is not met, the code inside the if block won't execute.

1.2 The else Statement

The else statement allows you to define an alternative action if the initial if condition is False. It always follows an if block.

Syntax:

```python
if condition:
    # Code if condition is True
else:
    # Code if condition is False
```

Example:

```python
age = 16
if age >= 18:
    print("You are eligible to vote.")
else:
    print("You are not eligible to vote yet.")
```

Here, the program will output "You are not eligible to vote yet." since age is not 18 or greater.

1.3 The elif Statement

The elif (short for "else if") statement allows you to add multiple conditions. Each elif checks its own condition if the previous if or elif conditions are False.

Syntax:

```python
if condition1:
    # Code if condition1 is True
elif condition2:
    # Code if condition2 is True
else:
    # Code if none of the above conditions are True
```

Example:

```python
score = 85
if score >= 90:
    print("Grade: A")
elif score >= 80:
    print("Grade: B")
else:
    print("Grade: C")
```

This code evaluates the score variable and prints the grade based on the value. Since score is 85, it matches the elif condition and outputs "Grade: B."

2. Logical Operators in Conditionals

When building conditions, you may need to combine multiple criteria. Python provides logical operators to help make these combinations:

- **and**: Both conditions must be True for the combined condition to be True.
- **or**: Only one of the conditions needs to be True for the combined condition to be True.
- **not**: Inverts the condition, making True False, and vice versa.

Example:

```python
temperature = 75
is_sunny = True
if temperature > 70 and is_sunny:
    print("It's a perfect day!")
```

In this case, both conditions (temperature > 70 and is_sunny) must be True for the message to print.

3. Loops

Loops allow for repeated execution of a block of code as long as a condition holds true. Python provides two primary types of loops: **while loops** and **for loops**.

3.1 The while Loop

A while loop executes a block of code as long as the specified condition evaluates to True. It's typically used when the number of iterations isn't known in advance.

Syntax:

```python
while condition:
    # Code to repeat while condition is True
```

Example:

```python
count = 0
while count < 5:
    print("Counting:", count)
    count += 1
```

In this example, the while loop continues to run as long as count is less than 5. The count += 1 statement increases the value of count by 1 in each iteration, so the loop eventually terminates.

Caution: If a while loop lacks a way to eventually make the condition False, it will result in an **infinite loop**, which runs indefinitely.

3.2 The for Loop

A for loop iterates over a sequence (like a list, tuple, or string) and executes a block of code once for each item in the sequence. This loop is useful when the number of iterations is known or when iterating over a collection.

Syntax:

```python
for item in sequence:
    # Code to execute for each item
```

Example:

```python
fruits = ["apple", "banana", "cherry"]
for fruit in fruits:
    print("I like", fruit)
```

This loop iterates over each element in the fruits list and prints a statement for each fruit.

4. The range() Function in Loops

Python's built-in range() function generates a sequence of numbers, which is particularly useful in for loops for controlling the number of iterations.

Syntax:

```python
range(start, stop, step)
```

- **start**: The starting number (inclusive). Defaults to 0 if omitted.
- **stop**: The endpoint (exclusive), where the range ends.
- **step**: The amount by which to increment. Defaults to 1.

Example:

```python
for i in range(1, 6):
    print("Number:", i)
```

In this example, i takes on values from 1 to 5 (as the stop value, 6, is not included).

5. Nested Loops and Conditional Statements

Both if statements and loops can be nested. Nested loops or conditionals allow for complex, multi-layered logic within your programs.

Example of Nested Conditional in a Loop:

```python
numbers = [1, 2, 3, 4, 5]
for number in numbers:
    if number % 2 == 0:
        print(number, "is even")
```

```
    else:
        print(number, "is odd")
```

This example iterates over a list of numbers and uses an if statement inside the for loop to check if each number is even or odd, printing the result for each.

6. Control Flow Tools in Loops: break and continue

Python provides additional tools to control loops: break and continue.

- **break**: Terminates the loop immediately, regardless of the loop condition.
- **continue**: Skips the current iteration and moves to the next one.

Example of break:

```python
for number in range(1, 10):
    if number == 5:
        break
    print(number)
```

In this example, the loop stops as soon as number equals 5, so only the numbers 1 through 4 are printed.

Example of continue:

```python
for number in range(1, 10):
    if number % 2 == 0:
        continue
    print(number)
```

This loop skips even numbers, printing only odd numbers from 1 to 9.

The continue statement causes the loop to skip the print() statement when number is even.

Understanding conditional statements and loops is essential for making your programs dynamic, responsive, and efficient. By mastering if, elif, and else statements, you can implement decision-making logic. Loops like while and for, along with control tools like break and continue, allow you to handle repetitive tasks and iterate over collections.

As you move into the coding challenges, practice using these structures in varied ways. Experiment with nesting, combining conditions, and using loop controls to gain confidence and versatility in coding with Python.

Challenge 11–20: If-Else Statements and Logic Building

Topics Covered: Basic conditions, nested if-else structures, and comparison operators.

In this set of challenges, you'll apply what you've learned about if-else statements, comparison operators, and logical structures to develop your decision-making skills in Python. Each challenge will provide practice with logic building, testing conditions, and using nested conditionals to handle more complex scenarios.

Challenge 11: Voting Eligibility Checker

Write a program that takes an integer input representing a person's age and determines if they are eligible to vote. If the person is 18 or older, print "Eligible to vote"; otherwise, print "Not eligible to vote."

Example Input: age = 20

Expected Output: Eligible to vote

Challenge 12: Grade Calculator

Create a program that calculates and prints a student's grade based on their score. The grading scale is as follows:

- 90 and above: Grade A
- 80 to 89: Grade B
- 70 to 79: Grade C
- Below 70: Grade D

Example Input: score = 85
Expected Output: Grade B

Challenge 13: Even or Odd Checker
Write a program that checks if a given integer is even or odd. If the number is even, print "Even"; if it's odd, print "Odd."
Example Input: number = 7
Expected Output: Odd

Challenge 14: Number Comparison
Develop a program that takes two integers as inputs and prints:

- "First is larger" if the first number is larger than the second.
- "Second is larger" if the second number is larger than the first.
- "Both are equal" if the two numbers are the same.

Example Input: num1 = 12, num2 = 10
Expected Output: First is larger

Challenge 15: Admission Eligibility
A college program has specific requirements for admission: the student's average score must be at least 85, and they must have a strong recommendation letter. Create a program that checks both conditions and prints:

- "Eligible for admission" if both conditions are met.
- "Not eligible for admission" if any condition is not met.

Example Input: average_score = 90, recommendation = True

Expected Output: Eligible for admission

Challenge 16: Triangle Type Checker
Write a program that takes three sides of a triangle as input and determines if the triangle is:

- Equilateral (all sides equal)
- Isosceles (two sides equal)
- Scalene (all sides different)

Example Input: side1 = 5, side2 = 5, side3 = 8
Expected Output: Isosceles

Challenge 17: Password Strength Checker
Create a program that checks the strength of a password based on the following criteria:

- If the password length is 8 or more and contains both numbers and letters, print "Strong password."
- Otherwise, print "Weak password."

Example Input: password = "Pass1234"
Expected Output: Strong password

Challenge 18: Day of the Week
Write a program that takes an integer from 1 to 7 representing the day of the week (1 for Monday, 2 for Tuesday, etc.) and prints the corresponding day. If the input is not between 1 and 7, print "Invalid input."
Example Input: day = 3
Expected Output: Wednesday

Challenge 19: Simple Calculator
Design a basic calculator that takes two numbers and an operator (+, -, *, /) as inputs and performs the operation on the two numbers. Print the

result.

Example Input: num1 = 8, num2 = 4, operator = '/'

Expected Output: 2

Challenge 20: Season Checker

Write a program that takes a month (1 for January, 2 for February, etc.) and prints the corresponding season:

- Winter (December, January, February)
- Spring (March, April, May)
- Summer (June, July, August)
- Fall (September, October, November)

Example Input: month = 4

Expected Output: Spring

Each of these challenges emphasizes the use of basic if-else statements, comparison operators, and logical structures. They are foundational exercises that will strengthen your logic-building abilities, making it easier to tackle more complex conditional scenarios.

Challenge 21–30: Loops and Iteration (for and while loops)

Topics Covered: Basics of for and while loops, nested loops, and control keywords (break and continue).

In these challenges, you'll explore the mechanics of loops, focusing on how to control repetitive tasks and manage iterations efficiently. These exercises will also introduce you to nested loops and special control keywords, helping you build complex logic within loops.

Challenge 21: Print Numbers from 1 to 10

Write a program that uses a for loop to print numbers from 1 to 10.

Expected Output:

```python
1
2
3
...
10
```

Challenge 22: Sum of First 50 Natural Numbers

Create a program that uses a while loop to calculate and print the sum of the first 50 natural numbers.

Expected Output: 1275

Challenge 23: Multiplication Table

Write a program that prints the multiplication table of a given number. Use a for loop to display the table up to 10.

Example Input: number = 5
Expected Output:

```python
5 x 1 = 5
5 x 2 = 10
...
5 x 10 = 50
```

Challenge 24: Factorial Calculator

Develop a program that calculates the factorial of a number entered by the user. Use a while loop for this calculation.

Example Input: number = 5
Expected Output: 120 (since 5! = 5 × 4 × 3 × 2 × 1)

Challenge 25: Even Numbers in a Range

Write a program that takes two integers as input (a start and an end) and prints all even numbers in that range. Use a for loop to check each number.

Example Input: start = 2, end = 10
Expected Output:

```
2
4
6
8
10
```

Challenge 26: Sum of Odd Numbers Between 1 and 100
Use a for loop to find the sum of all odd numbers between 1 and 100.
Expected Output: 2500

Challenge 27: Find Prime Numbers
Write a program that prints all prime numbers between 1 and 50. Use nested for loops to determine if each number is prime.
Expected Output:

```python
2
3
5
7
11
...
47
```

Challenge 28: Number Guessing Game
Create a simple number guessing game. The program randomly selects a number between 1 and 10, and the user has three attempts to guess it correctly. If the user guesses correctly, print "Congratulations! You've guessed the right number." If the guess is wrong after three attempts, print "Out of attempts."

Use a while loop for the guessing attempts and include a break statement if the user guesses correctly.

Challenge 29: Find Divisors of a Number

Write a program that takes an integer as input and finds all divisors of that number using a for loop.

Example Input: number = 12

Expected Output:

```
1
2
3
4
6
12
```

Challenge 30: Skip Multiples of 3

Using a for loop, print numbers from 1 to 20, but skip any number that is a multiple of

3. Use the continue keyword to skip these numbers.

Expected Output:

```python
1
2
4
5
7
8
10
...
19
```

Each of these challenges gives you hands-on practice with loops, conditions, and control structures in Python. As you work through them, pay attention to the logic required to set loop boundaries, manage nested iterations, and use break and continue effectively.

Solutions and Explanations for Challenges 21–30

Here are detailed solutions and explanations for each of the loop challenges in this section. Understanding these solutions will help reinforce your knowledge of loop structures and control flow in Python.

Challenge 21 Solution: Print Numbers from 1 to 10
Solution:

```python
for i in range(1, 11):
    print(i)
```

Explanation:

The range(1, 11) function generates numbers from 1 up to (but not including) 11, so it outputs numbers from 1 to 10. The for loop iterates over each number and prints it.

Challenge 22 Solution: Sum of First 50 Natural Numbers
Solution:

```python
sum = 0
i = 1
while i <= 50:
    sum += i
```

```
    i += 1
print(sum)
```

Explanation:

This while loop adds each number from 1 to 50 to the sum variable. The loop condition i <= 50 ensures that the loop stops once i exceeds 50. After the loop finishes, the final sum is printed.

Challenge 23 Solution: Multiplication Table
Solution:

```python
number = 5   # Example number
for i in range(1, 11):
    print(f"{number} x {i} = {number * i}")
```

Explanation:

The loop iterates from 1 to 10, multiplying number by i in each iteration. The result is formatted into a readable string using f-strings and then printed. Adjust number to get a table for any integer.

Challenge 24 Solution: Factorial Calculator
Solution:

```python
number = 5   # Example number
factorial = 1
while number > 1:
    factorial *= number
    number -= 1
print(factorial)
```

Explanation:

The while loop multiplies factorial by number in each iteration, decrementing number until it reaches 1. The factorial result is then printed. This solution works for any positive integer number.

Challenge 25 Solution: Even Numbers in a Range
Solution:

```python
start = 2
end = 10
for i in range(start, end + 1):
    if i % 2 == 0:
        print(i)
```

Explanation:

The loop iterates from start to end. The condition i % 2 == 0 checks if the number is even (if the remainder when divided by 2 is zero). Only even numbers are printed.

Challenge 26 Solution: Sum of Odd Numbers Between 1 and 100
Solution:

```python
sum = 0
for i in range(1, 101, 2):
    sum += i
print(sum)
```

Explanation:

By using range(1, 101, 2), we generate only odd numbers between 1 and 100, avoiding the need for additional checks within the loop. The loop sums up these odd numbers and prints the final result.

Challenge 27 Solution: Find Prime Numbers

Solution:

```python
for num in range(2, 51):
    is_prime = True
    for i in range(2, int(num ** 0.5) + 1):
        if num % i == 0:
            is_prime = False
            break
    if is_prime:
        print(num)
```

Explanation:

The outer loop iterates over each number from 2 to 50. For each num, we use a nested for loop to check if it is divisible by any number from 2 up to the square root of num (rounded up). If a divisor is found, is_prime is set to False, and the inner loop breaks. Only prime numbers are printed.

Challenge 28 Solution: Number Guessing Game
Solution:

```python
import random
target = random.randint(1, 10)
attempts = 3

while attempts > 0:
    guess = int(input("Guess a number between 1 and 10: "))
    if guess == target:
        print("Congratulations! You've guessed the right
        number.")
        break
    else:
        attempts -= 1
        print(f"Incorrect. You have {attempts} attempts left.")
```

```python
if attempts == 0:
    print(f"Out of attempts! The number was {target}.")
```

Explanation:

This program generates a random number from 1 to 10. The user has three attempts to guess it. The while loop runs until attempts reaches zero. If the guess matches target, the loop breaks, and a success message is printed. If not, the user is informed of the remaining attempts. After three wrong guesses, the correct answer is revealed.

Challenge 29 Solution: Find Divisors of a Number
Solution:

```python
number = 12  # Example number
for i in range(1, number + 1):
    if number % i == 0:
        print(i)
```

Explanation:

The loop iterates over each number from 1 to number. If number % i == 0, then i is a divisor of number, so it is printed. Adjust number to find divisors of any integer.

Challenge 30 Solution: Skip Multiples of 3
Solution:

```python
for i in range(1, 21):
    if i % 3 == 0:
        continue
```

```
print(i)
```

Explanation:

The loop iterates from 1 to 20. If i % 3 == 0, the continue statement skips the current iteration, so multiples of 3 aren't printed. The loop proceeds with the next number. This solution effectively filters out multiples of 3 from the output.

These solutions provide practical applications of loops, conditions, and control keywords (break and continue). By understanding these examples, you'll gain confidence in handling various loop-based logic problems in Python.

Mini Project 1: Number Guessing Game

In this mini-project, we'll build a complete **Number Guessing Game** in Python, designed to test and enhance your understanding of conditional statements, loops, and basic user input handling.

Project Objective

The goal is to create a game where the computer randomly selects a number within a specified range, and the player has a limited number of attempts to guess it. After each guess, the game provides feedback, helping the player narrow down possible answers. The game ends when the player either guesses correctly or runs out of attempts.

Project Requirements

1. **Randomly Select a Number**: Use Python's random module to generate a number between 1 and 100 (or any range you choose).
2. **User Input**: Prompt the player to enter a guess.
3. **Feedback for Each Guess**: After each guess, tell the player whether their guess is too high, too low, or correct.
4. **Limit the Number of Attempts**: The player should have a finite number of attempts (e.g., 7 attempts) to guess the number.

5. **Ending the Game**:

- If the player guesses correctly, display a congratulatory message.
- If the player runs out of attempts, reveal the correct number and end the game.

Step-by-Step Solution

1. **Import the Random Module**:

- We'll use random.randint() to generate a random number within our chosen range.

1. **Set Up Game Parameters**:

- Define the range of possible numbers (e.g., 1 to 100).
- Set the number of attempts allowed (e.g., 7).

1. **Create the Game Loop**:

- Use a while loop to keep the game running as long as the player has remaining attempts.
- For each iteration, prompt the player to enter a guess, check if it matches the randomly selected number, and give feedback based on whether the guess was too high, too low, or correct.

1. **Handle Win and Lose Conditions**:

- If the player guesses correctly, exit the loop and display a congratulatory message.
- If the player runs out of attempts, reveal the correct number.

Full Code Implementation

Here's the complete code for the **Number Guessing Game**:

```python
import random

# Step 1: Initialize game parameters
lower_bound = 1
upper_bound = 100
max_attempts = 7
target_number = random.randint(lower_bound, upper_bound)

# Step 2: Welcome message
print("Welcome to the Number Guessing Game!")
print(f"I'm thinking of a number between {lower_bound} and {upper_bound}.")
print(f"You have {max_attempts} attempts to guess it. Good luck!\n")

# Step 3: Game loop
attempts = 0
while attempts < max_attempts:
    # Step 4: Get user input
    try:
        guess = int(input(f"Attempt {attempts + 1}: Enter your guess: "))
    except ValueError:
        print("Please enter a valid integer.")
        continue

    # Step 5: Increment attempts
    attempts += 1

    # Step 6: Check if guess is correct
    if guess == target_number:
        print(f"Congratulations! You've guessed the correct number {target_number} in {attempts} attempts.")
        break
    elif guess < target_number:
        print("Too low! Try a higher number.")
```

```
    else:
        print("Too high! Try a lower number.")

    # Step 7: Check if attempts are exhausted
    if attempts == max_attempts:
        print(f"Sorry, you've run out of attempts. The correct
        number was {target_number}.")

print("Thank you for playing!")
```

Explanation of Key Parts

- **Generating the Target Number:**

python

```
target_number = random.randint(lower_bound, upper_bound)
```

- This line picks a random integer between lower_bound and upper_bound.
- **Getting User Input:**

python

```
guess = int(input(f"Attempt {attempts + 1}: Enter your guess: "))
```

- Here, the user is prompted to enter an integer guess. The int() function converts the input into an integer, which is then stored in guess. If the input isn't an integer, it triggers an exception, prompting the user to enter a valid integer.

- **Evaluating the Guess**:

python

```
if guess == target_number:
    print(f"Congratulations! You've guessed the correct number
    {target_number} in {attempts} attempts.")
    break
elif guess < target_number:
    print("Too low! Try a higher number.")
else:
    print("Too high! Try a lower number.")
```

- If the guess matches target_number, the player wins, and the loop is exited using break. If the guess is lower or higher than target_number, an appropriate hint is given.
- **Ending the Game**:

python

```
if attempts == max_attempts:
    print(f"Sorry, you've run out of attempts. The correct
    number was {target_number}.")
```

- After each iteration, we check if attempts have reached max_attempts. If they have, the game ends, and the correct number is revealed.

Testing and Enhancements

Once your basic game works, consider adding these features:

- **Difficulty Levels**: Allow the player to select difficulty levels that modify the range of numbers and the allowed attempts.

- **Replay Option**: After each game, prompt the user to play again without restarting the program.
- **Score Keeping**: Track the number of wins and losses if the user plays multiple rounds.

Sample Game Output

```vbnet
Welcome to the Number Guessing Game!
I'm thinking of a number between 1 and 100.
You have 7 attempts to guess it. Good luck!

Attempt 1: Enter your guess: 50
Too low! Try a higher number.

Attempt 2: Enter your guess: 75
Too high! Try a lower number.

Attempt 3: Enter your guess: 62
Congratulations! You've guessed the correct number 62 in 3 attempts.
Thank you for playing!
```

This project is a great way to practice handling user input, managing loops and conditions, and adding polish to a Python program. With this mini-game, you've now created a fully functional interactive program that's fun and reusable.

Test Your Knowledge: Quick Quiz on Control Flow

This quick quiz will test your understanding of Python's control flow structures, specifically conditional statements and loops. Each question is designed to reinforce core concepts, helping you to identify any areas that may need further review.

Question 1: Understanding if Statements

What will be the output of the following code?

```python
x = 10
if x > 5:
    print("Greater than 5")
if x > 8:
    print("Greater than 8")
if x > 12:
    print("Greater than 12")
```

Options:

1. Greater than 5
2. Greater than 5, Greater than 8
3. Greater than 5, Greater than 8, Greater than 12
4. No output

Answer:
Explanation: Each if statement is checked independently.

Question 2: Using else and elif

Consider the following code. What will be the output if score is set to 85?

```python
score = 85
if score >= 90:
    print("Grade: A")
elif score >= 80:
    print("Grade: B")
elif score >= 70:
    print("Grade: C")
else:
```

```python
print("Grade: F")
```

Options:

1. Grade: A
2. Grade: B
3. Grade: C
4. Grade: F

Answer:
Explanation: elif statements are evaluated in sequence until a condition is met.

Question 3: Looping with for and range()
What is the output of this code?

```python
for i in range(5):
    print(i)
```

Options:

1. 1 2 3 4 5
2. 0 1 2 3 4
3. 0 1 2 3 4 5
4. Error

Answer:
Explanation: range(5) generates numbers from 0 up to, but not including, 5.

Question 4: Using while Loops
How many times will "Hello" be printed?

```python
count = 0
while count < 3:
    print("Hello")
    count += 1
```

Options:

1. 1
2. 2
3. 3
4. Infinite loop

Answer:

Explanation: The while loop runs until count reaches 3, incrementing each time.

Question 5: The break Statement

What will be the output of the following code?

```python
for i in range(5):
    if i == 3:
        break
    print(i)
```

Options:

1. 0 1 2 3 4
2. 0 1 2 3
3. 0 1 2
4. No output

Answer:

Explanation: break terminates the loop when i equals 3.

Question 6: The continue Statement

What will be printed by the following code?

```python
for i in range(5):
    if i == 2:
        continue
    print(i)
```

Options:

1. 0 1 3 4
2. 0 1 2 3 4
3. 0 1
4. 0 1 2

Answer:

Explanation: continue skips the iteration when i equals 2.

Question 7: Nested Loops

How many times will the inner loop print "Inside Loop" in the following code?

```python
for i in range(3):
    for j in range(2):
        print("Inside Loop")
```

Options:

1. 3
2. 5
3. 6
4. 9

Answer:

Explanation: The inner loop runs twice for each iteration of the outer loop, resulting in 3 * 2 = 6 executions.

Question 8: Loop Control with else

What will be the output of the following code?

```python
for i in range(3):
    print(i)
else:
    print("Loop complete")
```

Options:

1. 0 1 2
2. 0 1 2 Loop complete
3. Loop complete
4. Error

Answer:

Explanation: When a for loop completes all iterations without a break, the else block is executed.

Question 9: Combining if, for, and break

What will be printed by this code?

```python
for i in range(5):
    if i == 3:
        print("Found 3")
        break
    print(i)
```

Options:

1. 0 1 2 Found 3
2. Found 3
3. 0 1 2 3
4. 0 1 2

Answer:

Explanation: print("Found 3") is executed when i equals 3, and break stops the loop immediately afterward.

Question 10: Checking for Prime Numbers

Consider this code for checking if a number is prime. What will be the output if num = 10?

```python
num = 10
is_prime = True
for i in range(2, num):
    if num % i == 0:
        is_prime = False
        break
if is_prime:
    print("Prime")
else:
    print("Not prime")
```

Options:

1. Prime
2. Not prime
3. 10 is a prime number
4. 10 is not a prime number

Answer:

Explanation: 10 is divisible by 2, so is_prime becomes False and Not prime is printed.

This quiz covers essential control flow concepts in Python, from conditionals and loops to using break and continue effectively. Review any questions you found challenging, as mastering these fundamentals is key to writing efficient, readable Python code.

Functions and Problem Decomposition

Overview: Breaking Down Code with Functions

In programming, functions are essential tools that allow us to organize, simplify, and reuse code. Functions enable developers to break down complex problems into manageable pieces, which can be individually developed, tested, and maintained. By isolating functionality, functions reduce redundancy, enhance readability, and facilitate troubleshooting and scaling applications. This chapter will introduce the concept of functions in Python, covering their structure, syntax, and best practices for using them effectively in problem-solving.

What is a Function?

A function in Python is a block of reusable code designed to perform a specific task. Functions encapsulate logic, taking inputs (parameters) and returning outputs, making the code more modular and organized. Functions are defined using Python's def keyword, followed by the function's name, parameter list (optional), and a colon. The body of the function, indented below, contains the code to execute.

Basic structure of a Python function:

```python
def function_name(parameters):
    # Code to execute
    return output  # Optional return statement
```

Example:

```python
def greet(name):
    return f"Hello, {name}!"
```

In this example, the greet function takes one parameter (name) and returns a greeting message customized with that name.

Why Use Functions?

1. **Code Reusability**: Functions can be called multiple times within a program, reducing duplication.
2. **Modularity**: Functions allow developers to break complex problems into smaller, manageable parts.
3. **Readability and Maintainability**: Named functions clarify the purpose of code blocks, making code easier to read and maintain.
4. **Testing and Debugging**: Isolated functions simplify debugging since each function can be tested independently.

Types of Functions

Python offers several types of functions, each serving different purposes:

- **Built-in Functions**: Predefined functions provided by Python (e.g., print(), len(), range()).
- **User-defined Functions**: Functions created by users to perform specific tasks.
- **Lambda Functions**: Anonymous, single-expression functions, useful for simple operations.

Defining and Calling Functions

To define a function, use the def keyword, followed by a function name that describes its purpose, parentheses for parameters, and a colon. Inside

FUNCTIONS AND PROBLEM DECOMPOSITION

the function, write the code block that defines its behavior. Finally, call the function by typing its name and passing required arguments.

Example:

```python
def add_numbers(a, b):
    return a + b

result = add_numbers(5, 7)  # Calls the function with arguments 5 and 7
print(result)  # Output: 12
```

In this example, add_numbers is a user-defined function that takes two arguments (a and b), adds them, and returns the result.

Parameters and Arguments

Functions often take inputs, called **parameters**, which allow for flexibility. When you call a function, the values you pass are called **arguments**. Parameters are defined within the parentheses of the function definition, while arguments are provided in the function call.

Example:

```python
def multiply(a, b):
    return a * b

product = multiply(4, 6)  # Here, 4 and 6 are arguments passed to parameters a and b
print(product)  # Output: 24
```

Types of Arguments

1. **Positional Arguments**: Matched by the order in which they're provided.

2. **Keyword Arguments**: Passed with a specific parameter name, allowing flexibility in order.
3. **Default Arguments**: Provide a default value if an argument isn't specified.

Example with default arguments:

```python
def greet(name, message="Hello"):
    return f"{message}, {name}!"

print(greet("Alice"))            # Output: Hello, Alice!
print(greet("Alice", "Welcome")) # Output: Welcome, Alice!
```

Return Statement

The return statement specifies the output of a function. Once a function reaches a return, it terminates and sends the specified value back to the caller. If no return statement is provided, Python returns None by default.
Example:

```python
def square(x):
    return x * x

result = square(5)
print(result)  # Output: 25
```

Scope and Lifetime of Variables

Variables defined within a function have **local scope**, meaning they are only accessible within that function. Once the function finishes, these variables are deleted, freeing up memory. Understanding scope is essential to avoid unintended behavior when using variables with the same name in different parts of your program.

Example:

```python
def sample_function():
    local_var = 10  # Only accessible within sample_function

sample_function()
print(local_var)  # Raises an error because local_var is not accessible outside the function
```

Python also supports **global variables**, which are accessible across the entire program. However, excessive use of global variables can lead to errors and is discouraged.

Function Composition and Problem Decomposition

In complex programs, it's essential to break down large tasks into smaller functions, each handling a single responsibility. This is known as **problem decomposition**. By dividing code into small, reusable functions, you make it more readable, easier to debug, and scalable.

Example: Suppose you want to calculate the area and circumference of a circle.

```python
import math

def area(radius):
    return math.pi * (radius ** 2)

def circumference(radius):
    return 2 * math.pi * radius

# Now, we can reuse these functions independently
print("Area:", area(5))
print("Circumference:", circumference(5))
```

By decomposing the problem, each function remains small and focused, improving readability and maintainability.

Best Practices for Using Functions

1. **Use Descriptive Names**: Function names should reflect their purpose.
2. **Keep Functions Focused**: Each function should perform a single, specific task.
3. **Avoid Side Effects**: Functions should ideally not change external variables or states.
4. **Comment Complex Logic**: If a function performs complex operations, consider adding comments explaining its behavior.
5. **Use Docstrings**: Docstrings provide a quick summary of the function's purpose, parameters, and return values.

Example with a docstring:

```python
def calculate_area(radius):
    """
    Calculate the area of a circle.

    Parameters:
    radius (float): The radius of the circle.

    Returns:
    float: The area of the circle.
    """
    return math.pi * (radius ** 2)
```

Common Mistakes to Avoid

1. **Missing return Statements**: Forgetting to return a value when one is expected can lead to unexpected None results.
2. **Incorrect Argument Order**: When using positional arguments,

FUNCTIONS AND PROBLEM DECOMPOSITION

passing them in the wrong order can cause bugs.
3. **Modifying Global Variables**: Avoid altering global variables within functions, as this can create unpredictable behavior.

Practical Application: Step-by-Step Problem Decomposition Example

Let's walk through an example to illustrate the power of functions in problem decomposition. Suppose you want to write a program that processes a list of student grades, calculating the average and determining if each student passed or failed.

Step 1: Define the Problem
We need to:

1. Calculate the average grade.
2. Check if each student passed (assuming a passing grade is 60 or higher).
3. Display results.

Step 2: Identify Tasks and Functions

- Function to calculate the average.
- Function to check if a grade is passing.
- Function to display results.

Step 3: Implement the Solution

```python
def calculate_average(grades):
    return sum(grades) / len(grades)

def is_passing(grade):
    return grade >= 60

def display_results(grades):
```

```python
    average = calculate_average(grades)
    print(f"Average Grade: {average}")

    for grade in grades:
        result = "Pass" if is_passing(grade) else "Fail"
        print(f"Grade: {grade} - {result}")

# Sample grades
grades = [85, 90, 76, 45, 67]
display_results(grades)
```

In this example:

- The calculate_average function isolates the logic for averaging grades.
- The is_passing function checks individual grades.
- The display_results function combines these steps and outputs the results.

Functions are the foundation of modular programming, enabling you to create organized, readable, and reusable code. By understanding how to define, call, and structure functions effectively, you can break down complex tasks, making them easier to manage and troubleshoot. Developing good habits with functions will make your code cleaner and more professional, laying a strong foundation for tackling larger programming challenges.

Challenge 31-40: Writing Simple Functions

In this section, we will explore a series of challenges designed to help you understand the fundamentals of defining functions, using parameters, and returning values. These exercises will build your proficiency in writing Python functions and solidify your understanding of function composition.

Challenge 31: A Function to Add Two Numbers

Task: Write a function named add_two_numbers that takes two parameters and returns their sum.

Example Input:
add_two_numbers(3, 5)

Example Output:
8

Solution:

python

```
def add_two_numbers(a, b):
    return a + b

# Test the function
print(add_two_numbers(3, 5))   # Output: 8
```

Challenge 32: Function for Subtraction

Task: Write a function named subtract_numbers that takes two parameters and returns the result of subtracting the second number from the first.

Example Input:
subtract_numbers(10, 4)

Example Output:
6

Solution:

python

```
def subtract_numbers(a, b):
    return a - b

# Test the function
print(subtract_numbers(10, 4))   # Output: 6
```

Challenge 33: Function to Calculate the Area of a Rectangle

Task: Write a function calculate_area that takes the width and height of a rectangle and returns the area.

Example Input:
calculate_area(5, 10)

Example Output:
50

Solution:

```python
def calculate_area(width, height):
    return width * height

# Test the function
print(calculate_area(5, 10))   # Output: 50
```

Challenge 34: Function to Check if a Number is Even

Task: Write a function is_even that takes a number as input and returns True if it is even and False if it is odd.

Example Input:
is_even(6)

Example Output:
True

Solution:

```python
def is_even(number):
    return number % 2 == 0

# Test the function
print(is_even(6))   # Output: True
print(is_even(7))   # Output: False
```

FUNCTIONS AND PROBLEM DECOMPOSITION

Challenge 35: Function to Find the Maximum of Two Numbers

Task: Write a function find_maximum that takes two numbers as input and returns the larger number.

Example Input:
find_maximum(4, 9)

Example Output:
9

Solution:

```python
def find_maximum(a, b):
    return a if a > b else b

# Test the function
print(find_maximum(4, 9))   # Output: 9
```

Challenge 36: Function to Convert Celsius to Fahrenheit

Task: Write a function celsius_to_fahrenheit that takes a temperature in Celsius and converts it to Fahrenheit.

Formula:

$F = (C * 9/5) + 32$

Example Input:
celsius_to_fahrenheit(0)

Example Output:
32.0

Solution:

```python
def celsius_to_fahrenheit(celsius):
    return (celsius * 9/5) + 32

# Test the function
```

```
print(celsius_to_fahrenheit(0))   # Output: 32.0
```

Challenge 37: Function to Calculate the Factorial of a Number

Task: Write a function factorial that takes a number as input and returns the factorial of that number.

Example Input:
factorial(5)

Example Output:
120

Solution:

python

```
def factorial(n):
    if n == 0 or n == 1:
        return 1
    else:
        return n * factorial(n - 1)

# Test the function
print(factorial(5))   # Output: 120
```

Challenge 38: Function to Count Vowels in a String

Task: Write a function count_vowels that takes a string as input and returns the number of vowels (a, e, i, o, u) in that string.

Example Input:
count_vowels("hello world")

Example Output:
3

Solution:

python

```
def count_vowels(s):
    vowels = "aeiou"
```

```
    count = 0
    for char in s:
        if char.lower() in vowels:
            count += 1
    return count

# Test the function
print(count_vowels("hello world"))  # Output: 3
```

Challenge 39: Function to Check for a Palindrome

Task: Write a function is_palindrome that takes a string as input and returns True if the string is a palindrome (a word, phrase, or sequence that reads the same backward as forward) and False otherwise.

Example Input:
is_palindrome("madam")

Example Output:
True

Solution:

python

```
def is_palindrome(s):
    return s == s[::-1]

# Test the function
print(is_palindrome("madam"))  # Output: True
print(is_palindrome("hello"))  # Output: False
```

Challenge 40: Function to Return the Length of a String

Task: Write a function string_length that takes a string as input and returns its length.

Example Input:
string_length("Python")

Example Output: 6

Solution:

```python
def string_length(s):
    return len(s)

# Test the function
print(string_length("Python"))   # Output: 6
```

Summary of Key Concepts Covered:

1. **Function Definitions**: You've learned how to define functions in Python using the def keyword, along with using parameters and the return statement.
2. **Parameter Usage**: Understanding how to pass data into functions and use it within the function body is crucial. You explored both positional and keyword parameters.
3. **Returning Values**: Functions can return values, which can then be used in the program, further highlighting the modular nature of functions.
4. **Common Use Cases**: These challenges cover common Python use cases such as arithmetic operations, string manipulations, and condition-based logic, all of which demonstrate how to apply functions to real-world problems.

Completing these challenges will not only boost your understanding of function creation but also help you to build more organized, reusable, and readable code as you move forward with more complex projects.

Challenge 41–50: Applying Functions to Real Problems

In this section, we will delve deeper into more complex function challenges. These challenges are designed to introduce concepts like function scope, default parameters, and function chaining. By applying functions to real-world problems, you'll gain a better understanding of

FUNCTIONS AND PROBLEM DECOMPOSITION

how functions work in practice and how to use them effectively in larger projects.

Challenge 41: Function Scope and Variable Accessibility

Task: Write two functions. The first function, set_value, assigns a value to a global variable. The second function, get_value, returns the value of that global variable. Demonstrate how the value set by set_value is accessible in get_value.

Example Input:
set_value(10)
get_value()

Example Output:
10

Solution:

```python
# Global variable
value = 0

def set_value(val):
    global value
    value = val

def get_value():
    return value

# Test the functions
set_value(10)
print(get_value())  # Output: 10
```

Explanation: In this example, the set_value function modifies a global variable value. The get_value function retrieves this global variable, showing how function scope works. The global keyword is used to indicate that value refers to the global variable, not a local one.

Challenge 42: Function with Default Parameters

Task: Write a function greet that takes a name as a parameter and returns a greeting message. Make the name parameter optional, using a default value of "Guest" if no name is provided.

Example Input:
greet("Alice")
greet()
Example Output:
"Hello, Alice!"
"Hello, Guest!"
Solution:

```python
def greet(name="Guest"):
    return f"Hello, {name}!"

# Test the function
print(greet("Alice"))   # Output: Hello, Alice!
print(greet())          # Output: Hello, Guest!
```

Explanation: The greet function uses a default parameter (name="Guest"), which is applied when no argument is provided. This allows the function to be more flexible, adapting to different use cases.

Challenge 43: Function Chaining with Multiple Return Values

Task: Write a function multiply that takes two numbers as arguments, multiplies them, and returns the result. Then, create another function divide that divides two numbers and returns the result. Use function chaining to call these functions sequentially and perform both operations on two numbers.

Example Input:
multiply(5, 2)
divide(10, 2)
Example Output:
10
5.0

Solution:

```python
def multiply(a, b):
    return a * b

def divide(a, b):
    return a / b

# Test function chaining
result = divide(multiply(5, 2), 2)
print(result)   # Output: 5.0
```

Explanation: Function chaining allows the output of one function to serve as the input for another function. In this example, the multiply function is called first, and its result is passed to the divide function.

Challenge 44: Function to Calculate the Total Price of Items with Tax

Task: Write a function calculate_total that takes the price of an item and a tax rate as arguments. It should return the total price of the item after applying the tax. Include a default tax rate of 10% if no tax rate is provided.

Example Input:
calculate_total(100)
calculate_total(100, 15)

Example Output:
110.0
115.0

Solution:

```python
def calculate_total(price, tax_rate=0.10):
    return price + (price * tax_rate)
```

```
# Test the function
print(calculate_total(100))        # Output: 110.0
print(calculate_total(100, 0.15))  # Output: 115.0
```

Explanation: This function calculates the total price by applying a tax rate, with a default value of 0.10 (10%). If no tax rate is provided, the default is used.

Challenge 45: Function to Reverse a String

Task: Write a function reverse_string that takes a string as input and returns the string reversed.

Example Input:
reverse_string("Python")

Example Output:
"nohtyP"

Solution:

```python

def reverse_string(s):
    return s[::-1]

# Test the function
print(reverse_string("Python"))  # Output: nohtyP
```

Explanation: The function uses Python's slicing feature to reverse the string. s[::-1] creates a new string by reversing the order of characters.

Challenge 46: Function to Count the Occurrences of a Character in a String

Task: Write a function count_char that takes a string and a character as input, and returns the number of occurrences of that character in the string.

Example Input:

count_char("hello world", "o")
Example Output:
2
Solution:

```python
def count_char(s, char):
    return s.count(char)

# Test the function
print(count_char("hello world", "o"))  # Output: 2
```

Explanation: The count_char function uses Python's built-in count method for strings, which returns the number of occurrences of a specified substring.

Challenge 47: Function to Find the Average of a List of Numbers

Task: Write a function find_average that takes a list of numbers and returns their average.
Example Input:
find_average([2, 4, 6, 8])
Example Output:
5.0
Solution:

```python
def find_average(numbers):
    return sum(numbers) / len(numbers)

# Test the function
print(find_average([2, 4, 6, 8]))  # Output: 5.0
```

Explanation: The function calculates the average by summing all elements in the list and dividing by the length of the list. It uses Python's built-in sum() function.

Challenge 48: Function to Remove Duplicates from a List

Task: Write a function remove_duplicates that takes a list as input and returns a new list with duplicate values removed.
Example Input:
remove_duplicates([1, 2, 2, 3, 4, 4])
Example Output:
[1, 2, 3, 4]
Solution:

```python
def remove_duplicates(lst):
    return list(set(lst))

# Test the function
print(remove_duplicates([1, 2, 2, 3, 4, 4]))  # Output: [1, 2, 3, 4]
```

Explanation: This function leverages Python's set data structure, which automatically removes duplicates. The result is then converted back to a list.

Challenge 49: Function to Check if a Number is Prime

Task: Write a function is_prime that takes a number as input and returns True if it is a prime number and False otherwise.
Example Input:
is_prime(7)
is_prime(10)
Example Output:
True
False
Solution:

FUNCTIONS AND PROBLEM DECOMPOSITION

```python
def is_prime(n):
    if n <= 1:
        return False
    for i in range(2, int(n ** 0.5) + 1):
        if n % i == 0:
            return False
    return True

# Test the function
print(is_prime(7))   # Output: True
print(is_prime(10))  # Output: False
```

Explanation: The function checks if a number is prime by attempting to divide it by all integers up to the square root of the number. If any division results in a remainder of 0, the number is not prime.

Challenge 50: Function to Create a Simple Countdown Timer

Task: Write a function countdown_timer that takes an integer representing seconds and counts down to zero, printing each second.

Example Input:
countdown_timer(5)

Example Output:
5 4 3 2 1 Time's up!

Solution:

```python
import time

def countdown_timer(seconds):
    while seconds > 0:
        print(seconds)
```

```
        time.sleep(1)    # Wait for 1 second before printing the
        next number
        seconds -= 1
    print("Time's up!")

# Test the function
countdown_timer(5)
```

Explanation: The function uses a while loop to decrement the seconds value until it reaches zero, printing each second. The time.sleep(1) function pauses execution for 1 second between each print.

Function Scope: Understanding the difference between local and global scope and how to use global variables within functions.

1. **Default Parameters**: Functions can be designed with default parameter values, making them more flexible and easier to use in different scenarios.
2. **Function Chaining**: By returning values from one function and passing them as arguments to another, you can create efficient workflows and streamline your code.
3. **Real-World Applications**: These challenges provided a variety of functions for solving common programming problems, from string manipulations to mathematical operations, giving you practical experience with Python functions.

By now, you should be able to write more complex functions and apply them to real-world problems, making your code more modular, reusable, and efficient.

Solutions and Explanations for Challenge 41–50

This section presents detailed solutions and explanations for each challenge, focusing on how to leverage function features such as scope, default parameters, and chaining to solve real-world programming problems.

Solution 41: Function Scope and Variable Accessibility

Explanation:
In this challenge, the functions set_value and get_value demonstrate how function scope works in Python. We declare value as a global variable outside the functions. In set_value, the global keyword is used to modify the global variable value. When get_value is called, it accesses the same value, showing how the global scope can persist across different functions.

Code:

```python
# Global variable
value = 0

def set_value(val):
    global value
    value = val

def get_value():
    return value

# Test
set_value(10)
print(get_value())  # Output: 10
```

Key Concept: This solution illustrates the use of the global keyword to access and modify a variable outside a function's local scope.

Solution 42: Function with Default Parameters

Explanation:
Here, greet has an optional parameter name, set to a default value of "Guest". If greet is called without a parameter, "Guest" is used automatically, making the function adaptable and user-friendly.

Code:

```python
```

```python
def greet(name="Guest"):
    return f"Hello, {name}!"

# Test
print(greet("Alice"))   # Output: Hello, Alice!
print(greet())          # Output: Hello, Guest!
```

Key Concept: Using default parameters in Python functions allows for flexible function calls and can reduce the need for extra parameters.

Solution 43: Function Chaining with Multiple Return Values
Explanation:

Function chaining is demonstrated by first calling multiply, whose result is passed to divide. This approach minimizes extra variables and allows for a more streamlined calculation process.

Code:

```python
def multiply(a, b):
    return a * b

def divide(a, b):
    return a / b

# Test
result = divide(multiply(5, 2), 2)
print(result)  # Output: 5.0
```

Key Concept: Function chaining is useful for simplifying complex operations by feeding one function's output directly into another.

Solution 44: Function to Calculate the Total Price of Items with Tax
Explanation:

The calculate_total function computes an item's price after tax. With tax_rate set to a default of 0.10, the function can handle both custom and default tax rates.

Code:

FUNCTIONS AND PROBLEM DECOMPOSITION

```python
def calculate_total(price, tax_rate=0.10):
    return price + (price * tax_rate)

# Test
print(calculate_total(100))        # Output: 110.0
print(calculate_total(100, 0.15))  # Output: 115.0
```

Key Concept: Default parameters simplify function usage when there's a commonly used value, like a standard tax rate.

Solution 45: Function to Reverse a String
Explanation:
The reverse_string function utilizes slicing to reverse the string efficiently, showcasing Python's ability to handle string operations concisely.

Code:

```python
def reverse_string(s):
    return s[::-1]

# Test
print(reverse_string("Python"))  # Output: nohtyP
```

Key Concept: String slicing is a powerful technique for manipulating strings with minimal code.

Solution 46: Function to Count the Occurrences of a Character in a String
Explanation:
This function uses the count method to identify the frequency of a specified character in a string. The built-in count method simplifies the process significantly.

Code:

```python
def count_char(s, char):
    return s.count(char)

# Test
print(count_char("hello world", "o"))  # Output: 2
```

Key Concept: Python's built-in methods often provide the most efficient solutions for string operations.

Solution 47: Function to Find the Average of a List of Numbers

Explanation:

The find_average function calculates the average by summing the list and dividing by its length. This approach demonstrates how Python can handle basic mathematical operations on lists.

Code:

```python
def find_average(numbers):
    return sum(numbers) / len(numbers)

# Test
print(find_average([2, 4, 6, 8]))  # Output: 5.0
```

Key Concept: The sum() function and list length provide a simple way to calculate averages.

Solution 48: Function to Remove Duplicates from a List

Explanation:

To remove duplicates, remove_duplicates converts the list to a set, which eliminates any duplicates. Converting it back to a list maintains the function's return type.

Code:

FUNCTIONS AND PROBLEM DECOMPOSITION

```python
def remove_duplicates(lst):
    return list(set(lst))

# Test
print(remove_duplicates([1, 2, 2, 3, 4, 4]))  # Output: [1, 2, 3, 4]
```

Key Concept: Using a set is a quick and easy way to remove duplicates from a list.

Solution 49: Function to Check if a Number is Prime
Explanation:
The is_prime function checks if a number is prime by iterating up to its square root. If any divisor leaves a remainder of zero, the number is not prime.

Code:

```python
def is_prime(n):
    if n <= 1:
        return False
    for i in range(2, int(n ** 0.5) + 1):
        if n % i == 0:
            return False
    return True

# Test
print(is_prime(7))   # Output: True
print(is_prime(10))  # Output: False
```

Key Concept: Limiting the iteration range to the square root of n optimizes the prime-checking process.

Solution 50: Function to Create a Simple Countdown Timer
Explanation:
The countdown_timer function uses a while loop to count down from a specified number of seconds. The time.sleep(1) function pauses for 1 second at each iteration, creating a real-time countdown.
Code:

```python
import time

def countdown_timer(seconds):
    while seconds > 0:
        print(seconds)
        time.sleep(1)
        seconds -= 1
    print("Time's up!")

# Test
countdown_timer(5)
```

Key Concept: Using time.sleep() with a loop allows for precise time-based actions in Python.

1. **Function Scope and Global Variables**: Access and modify global variables within functions.
2. **Default Parameters**: Simplify functions by providing default values, reducing the need for extra arguments.
3. **Function Chaining**: Integrate multiple functions to streamline processes.
4. **Built-in Methods**: Take advantage of Python's built-in methods for string and list operations.
5. **Real-World Problem Solving**: Applied programming tasks to simulate practical scenarios.

These solutions illustrate foundational Python programming concepts, enhancing your ability to create efficient, real-world applications using functions.

Mini Project 2: "Calculator Program with Functions"

In this mini-project, we'll build a versatile calculator program that performs basic arithmetic operations—addition, subtraction, multiplication, and division—through the use of modular functions. This project allows you to apply your knowledge of function definitions, parameters, and return values, as well as to enhance your skills in creating a user-friendly program. By the end of this project, you'll have a fully functional calculator that can take user input, perform calculations, and display results.

Project Requirements

The calculator program will include the following features:

1. **Four Basic Operations**: The program will support addition, subtraction, multiplication, and division.
2. **User Input**: It will take input for two numbers and the operation to perform.
3. **Function Modularity**: Each arithmetic operation will be defined in its own function to allow clear structure and modularity.
4. **Error Handling**: The program will handle invalid inputs (e.g., dividing by zero) gracefully.
5. **Looping Mechanism**: It will offer the option to perform multiple calculations in a single session.

Step 1: Define the Functions for Arithmetic Operations

Each arithmetic operation will be encapsulated in its own function. This modular approach allows for easy expansion if you want to add more functionality later.

- **Addition Function**

python

```
def add(x, y):
    return x + y
```

- **Subtraction Function**

python

```
def subtract(x, y):
    return x - y
```

- **Multiplication Function**

python

```
def multiply(x, y):
    return x * y
```

- **Division Function**

python

```
def divide(x, y):
    # Check for division by zero
    if y == 0:
        return "Error: Cannot divide by zero"
    return x / y
```

FUNCTIONS AND PROBLEM DECOMPOSITION

Each of these functions takes two parameters, x and y, and returns the result of the corresponding operation. The division function includes a condition to check for division by zero, which is a common error in calculators.

Step 2: Create a User Interface Function

This function will prompt the user to choose an operation and input two numbers. It will display the result of the calculation and then ask if the user wants to perform another calculation.

```python
def calculator():
    print("Welcome to the Calculator Program")
    print("Available operations:")
    print("1. Addition (+)")
    print("2. Subtraction (-)")
    print("3. Multiplication (*)")
    print("4. Division (/)")

    while True:
        # Take input from the user
        operation = input("Enter operation (+, -, *, /) or 'q'
        to quit: ")

        if operation == 'q':
            print("Exiting Calculator. Goodbye!")
            break

        if operation not in ['+', '-', '*', '/']:
            print("Invalid operation. Please select a valid
            operation.")
            continue

        try:
            num1 = float(input("Enter first number: "))
            num2 = float(input("Enter second number: "))
        except ValueError:
            print("Invalid input. Please enter numerical
```

```
        values.")
        continue

    # Perform the selected operation
    if operation == '+':
        result = add(num1, num2)
    elif operation == '-':
        result = subtract(num1, num2)
    elif operation == '*':
        result = multiply(num1, num2)
    elif operation == '/':
        result = divide(num1, num2)

    print(f"The result is: {result}")

    # Ask if the user wants another calculation
    cont = input("Would you like to perform another
    calculation? (yes/no): ").lower()
    if cont != 'yes':
        print("Exiting Calculator. Goodbye!")
        break
```

Explanation of the Code

1. **Operation Selection**: The calculator() function starts by displaying a menu of operations and prompts the user to choose one. If the user enters 'q', the program exits.
2. **User Input**: After the operation is chosen, the program requests two numbers from the user. Using float() allows the program to handle both integer and decimal inputs.
3. **Error Handling**: The try and except block catches any non-numerical input and prompts the user to enter valid numbers.
4. **Executing Operations**: Based on the selected operation, the appropriate function (add, subtract, multiply, divide) is called. The divide function has an additional check for division by zero to prevent runtime errors.
5. **Looping Mechanism**: The program uses a while loop, allowing users

to perform multiple calculations without restarting the program. After each calculation, it asks if the user wants to continue or exit.

Sample Run

Here's an example of how the program might work in a real session:

```vbnet
Welcome to the Calculator Program
Available operations:
1. Addition (+)
2. Subtraction (-)
3. Multiplication (*)
4. Division (/)
Enter operation (+, -, *, /) or 'q' to quit: +
Enter first number: 5
Enter second number: 10
The result is: 15.0
Would you like to perform another calculation? (yes/no): yes

Enter operation (+, -, *, /) or 'q' to quit: /
Enter first number: 20
Enter second number: 0
The result is: Error: Cannot divide by zero
Would you like to perform another calculation? (yes/no): no
Exiting Calculator. Goodbye!
```

- **Function Definitions**: Each operation is encapsulated in a function, demonstrating the power of modular programming.
- **Control Flow**: The program uses if-elif statements to control which operation is performed based on user input.
- **Error Handling**: try-except blocks manage invalid user input, and specific error handling in the division function prevents division by zero.
- **Loops and Conditional Statements**: The while loop enables the

program to continue until the user chooses to exit, making it interactive and user-friendly.

This project solidifies the fundamentals of function usage, input handling, and error management, creating a practical and reusable calculator program. After completing this project, you should feel more comfortable writing and organizing functions, especially for user-interactive applications.

Test Your Knowledge: Function-Related Quiz

This short quiz tests your understanding of function fundamentals, including function definitions, parameters, return values, scope, and function chaining. Answer the questions below to reinforce what you've learned in this chapter.

Question 1: What is the purpose of the return statement in a function?

- A) It prints the function's result to the screen.
- B) It exits the function without returning a value.
- C) It specifies the value that will be returned to the caller of the function.
- D) It is only used for debugging purposes.

Answer:

Question 2: Which of the following is the correct way to define a function in Python?

- A) function myFunc() {}
- B) def myFunc:
- C) def myFunc():
- D) func myFunc() {}

Answer:

FUNCTIONS AND PROBLEM DECOMPOSITION

Question 3: What will be the output of the following code?

```python
def add(a, b=5):
    return a + b

result = add(3)
print(result)
```

- A) 3
- B) 5
- C) 8
- D) This code will cause an error

Answer:

Question 4: When using the global keyword inside a function, which of the following happens?

- A) The variable is treated as a local variable within the function
- B) The variable is modified globally, affecting its value outside the function.
- C) The variable is converted to a string.
- D) The global keyword has no effect.

Answer:

Question 5: Which of these functions will return the string in reverse order?

```python
def reverse_string(s):
    return ___
```

- A) return s.reverse()
- B) return s[::-1]
- C) return s[:-1]
- D) return s.reverse_string()

Answer:

Question 6: In Python, what does def stand for, and how is it used?

- A) def is used to define a variable.
- B) def stands for "define function" and is used to create a new function.
- C) def is short for "default" and is used for setting default values.
- D) def is used for defining a loop.

Answer:

Question 7: What will be the output of the following code?

```python
def func(x, y):
    x += 5
    y *= 2
    return x, y

a, b = func(2, 3)
print(a, b)
```

- A) 7 6
- B) 2 3
- C) 10 5
- D) 5 6

Answer:

Question 8: Consider the following code:

```python
def outer_func():
    outer_var = "I am outer"

    def inner_func():
        nonlocal outer_var
        outer_var = "I am modified"

    inner_func()
    return outer_var

print(outer_func())
```

What is the output, and why?

- A) I am outer, because the inner function does not change the outer variable.
- B) I am modified, because the inner function uses nonlocal to modify the variable from the outer function.
- C) An error, because nonlocal can only be used for global variables.
- D) None of the above.

Answer:

Question 9: Which of these correctly demonstrates function chaining?

```python
def multiply_by_two(x):
    return x * 2

def add_three(x):
    return x + 3
```

- A) result = multiply_by_two(add_three(4))

- B) result = multiply_by_two add_three(4)
- C) result = multiply_by_two; add_three(4)
- D) result = add_three(multiply_by_two)

Answer:

Question 10: When would you use a default parameter in a function?

- A) To ensure a variable is always treated as global.
- B) To avoid defining a new variable.
- C) To provide a standard value for a parameter if none is supplied.
- D) To chain functions together.

Answer:

Quiz Review

After completing these questions, check your answers to confirm your understanding of Python functions. This quiz has covered key function-related topics that are essential for writing modular, flexible, and efficient code.

Mastering Data Structures (Lists, Tuples, Sets, Dictionaries)

Overview: Choosing the Right Data Structure

Data structures are foundational to writing efficient, scalable, and organized code. Each data structure—lists, tuples, sets, and dictionaries—offers unique strengths and is optimized for different types of operations, such as storing ordered data, managing unique elements, or associating keys with values. Understanding how and when to use each structure allows you to select the optimal one based on your task's requirements, impacting both the performance and readability of your code.

This chapter provides an in-depth look at these core data structures, exploring their syntax, key methods, and best practices. Let's begin by understanding the characteristics, common uses, and distinctions of each structure.

Lists: Ordered, Mutable Collections

A list is one of Python's most versatile data structures. Defined using square brackets [], lists are ordered collections of elements that can be modified after creation. Lists allow duplicate items, making them ideal for storing sequences where order and mutability are required.

Key Characteristics of Lists:

- **Order**: Elements retain the order in which they were added.

- **Mutability**: Lists can be changed, meaning you can add, remove, or modify elements.
- **Indexing**: Each element has an index, allowing fast access to specific items.

Common Uses of Lists:

- **Storing Ordered Data**: Use lists for ordered collections, such as daily tasks or steps in a process.
- **Dynamic Data Storage**: Lists are excellent for scenarios where data will change frequently.

Basic Syntax and Example:

```python
# Creating a list
fruits = ['apple', 'banana', 'cherry']

# Accessing elements by index
print(fruits[1])   # Output: 'banana'

# Modifying an element
fruits[0] = 'orange'   # Changes 'apple' to 'orange'

# Adding and removing elements
fruits.append('grape')
fruits.remove('banana')
```

When to Use Lists: Use lists when you need an ordered, changeable sequence of elements, especially if the sequence may contain duplicates or needs frequent modification.

Tuples: Ordered, Immutable Collections

Tuples are similar to lists but are immutable, meaning that once created, their elements cannot be changed. Defined using parentheses (), tuples offer a fast, memory-efficient way to store fixed sequences of items. Tuples also maintain the order of elements but do not support modification, making them ideal for data that should remain constant.

Key Characteristics of Tuples:

- **Order**: Like lists, tuples maintain order.
- **Immutability**: Elements cannot be added, removed, or changed after the tuple is created.
- **Indexing**: Elements can be accessed via index.

Common Uses of Tuples:

- **Fixed Data Collections**: Use tuples for data that shouldn't change, like geographical coordinates or settings configurations.
- **Returning Multiple Values**: Often used to return multiple values from a function in a single, immutable package.

Basic Syntax and Example:

```python
# Creating a tuple
coordinates = (10.0, 20.0)

# Accessing elements by index
print(coordinates[0])  # Output: 10.0

# Attempting to modify will raise an error
# coordinates[0] = 15.0  # TypeError
```

When to Use Tuples: Choose tuples when you need an ordered collection that should not change, offering memory efficiency and protecting data integrity.

Sets: Unordered, Unique Collections

Sets are unordered collections that do not allow duplicate elements. Defined using curly braces {}, sets are optimized for membership tests and deduplication. They are ideal for storing collections of unique items and supporting mathematical set operations, such as union and intersection.

Key Characteristics of Sets:

- **Unordered**: Sets do not maintain order.
- **No Duplicates**: Sets automatically remove duplicate values.
- **Mutable**: Elements can be added or removed, although the set itself does not support indexing or slicing.

Common Uses of Sets:

- **Unique Collections**: Ideal for removing duplicates from a list.
- **Membership Testing**: Sets provide fast membership checks, useful in scenarios like filtering.

Basic Syntax and Example:

```python
# Creating a set
unique_numbers = {1, 2, 3, 4, 4, 5}  # Duplicate '4' will be removed

# Adding and removing elements
unique_numbers.add(6)
unique_numbers.remove(2)

# Membership testing
print(3 in unique_numbers)  # Output: True
```

When to Use Sets: Use sets when you need to enforce uniqueness, perform fast membership checks, or handle mathematical set operations, such as unions and intersections.

Dictionaries: Key-Value Pair Collections

Dictionaries are collections of key-value pairs, defined using curly braces {} and colons : to separate keys and values. Unlike lists, dictionaries do not use numerical indexing; instead, each element (or "item") is accessed via a unique key. This structure is ideal for storing and quickly retrieving data based on custom identifiers.

Key Characteristics of Dictionaries:

- **Key-Value Pairs**: Each item is stored as a key: value pair.
- **Mutability**: Dictionaries can be modified by adding, removing, or updating items.
- **Unique Keys**: Keys must be unique and are typically strings or numbers.

Common Uses of Dictionaries:

- **Mapping Data**: Ideal for associating unique identifiers (like user IDs) with specific data (like user profiles).
- **Structured Data Storage**: Great for JSON-like structures, configurations, or any structured data.

Basic Syntax and Example:

```python
# Creating a dictionary
student = {'name': 'Alice', 'age': 20, 'major': 'Physics'}

# Accessing and modifying values by key
print(student['name'])   # Output: 'Alice'
student['age'] = 21      # Update the age

# Adding and removing items
student['graduated'] = False
```

```
del student['major']
```

When to Use Dictionaries: Choose dictionaries for data that needs to be accessed via unique identifiers, especially when data is structured and benefits from key-value pairing.

Summary of Data Structure Selection

Data Structure	Characteristics	Best Used For
List	Ordered, mutable, allows duplicates	Storing ordered sequences, frequently modified collections
Tuple	Ordered, immutable, allows duplicates	Fixed collections, function return values, constants
Set	Unordered, mutable, no duplicates	Unique collections, membership testing, set operations
Dictionary	Unordered (from Python 3.7+ retains insertion order), mutable, unique keys	Key-value mapping, structured data retrieval via unique identifiers

Choosing the right data structure hinges on understanding your data's requirements: if you need order and mutability, lists are ideal; if you need immutability and order, tuples are the way to go. For uniqueness, sets provide a robust solution, while dictionaries offer unparalleled efficiency for key-based data retrieval. By selecting the appropriate data structure, you enhance the efficiency, readability, and scalability of your Python programs.

Challenge 51-60: Working with Lists and Tuples

In this section, you'll deepen your understanding of lists and tuples through a series of challenges. These exercises focus on indexing, slicing, immutability, and list comprehensions—key concepts for manipulating data efficiently.

Challenge 51: Accessing Elements in a List

Objective: Given a list of student names, write a function that returns the third student in the list.

```python
# Example Input
students = ['Alice', 'Bob', 'Charlie', 'David', 'Eve']

# Expected Output
# 'Charlie'
```

Hint: Remember that indexing starts at 0 in Python. The third item in the list will have an index of 2.

Challenge 52: Slicing a List

Objective: Create a function that takes a list of numbers and returns a new list containing only the first half of the elements.

```python
# Example Input
numbers = [10, 20, 30, 40, 50, 60]

# Expected Output
# [10, 20, 30]
```

Hint: Use slicing to select a subset of the list. You can calculate the midpoint by dividing the length of the list by 2.

Challenge 53: Reverse a List Using Slicing

Objective: Write a function that takes a list of strings and returns the list in reverse order using slicing.

```python
# Example Input
words = ['Python', 'Java', 'C++', 'Ruby']

# Expected Output
# ['Ruby', 'C++', 'Java', 'Python']
```

Hint: Negative step values in slicing can reverse the order of elements.

Challenge 54: Using List Comprehension

Objective: Create a list of the squares of all even numbers between 1 and 20 using list comprehension.

```python
# Expected Output
# [4, 16, 36, 64, 100, 144, 196, 256, 324, 400]
```

Hint: Use a condition in your list comprehension to check if each number is even, and then square it if it meets the condition.

Challenge 55: Find the Maximum Value in a Tuple

Objective: Write a function that takes a tuple of integers and returns the maximum value.

```python
# Example Input
numbers = (3, 5, 7, 2, 8, 1)

# Expected Output
# 8
```

Hint: Use Python's built-in max() function, which works with tuples as well.

Challenge 56: Convert a Tuple to a List

Objective: Write a function that takes a tuple and converts it into a list.

```python
# Example Input
my_tuple = (1, 2, 3, 4)

# Expected Output
```

```
# [1, 2, 3, 4]
```

Hint: Use the list() function to transform the tuple.

Challenge 57: Tuple Immutability

Objective: Given a tuple of colors, write a function that attempts to change the first color and observe what happens.

```python
# Example Input
colors = ('red', 'green', 'blue')

# Expected Output
# TypeError indicating that tuples are immutable
```

Hint: Remember, tuples are immutable, meaning you cannot modify their elements after creation. Test what happens if you try modifying an element.

Challenge 58: List Comprehension with Conditionals

Objective: Given a list of integers, use list comprehension to create a new list containing only the odd numbers from the original list.

```python
# Example Input
numbers = [1, 2, 3, 4, 5, 6, 7, 8, 9]

# Expected Output
# [1, 3, 5, 7, 9]
```

Hint: Use a conditional within the list comprehension to filter out the even numbers.

Challenge 59: Sum All Elements in a Tuple

Objective: Write a function that takes a tuple of integers and returns the sum of all elements.

```python
# Example Input
my_tuple = (10, 20, 30, 40)

# Expected Output
# 100
```

Hint: Use Python's built-in sum() function, which works directly with tuples.

Challenge 60: Find the Index of an Element in a List

Objective: Write a function that takes a list and a target value, returning the index of the first occurrence of the target. If the target is not found, return -1.

```python
# Example Input
fruits = ['apple', 'banana', 'cherry', 'apple']
target = 'cherry'

# Expected Output
# 2
```

Hint: Use the .index() method, which is available for lists, but handle cases where the target is not found to avoid errors.

These challenges cover core techniques for working with lists and tuples, emphasizing how to access, manipulate, and filter data using Python's syntax.

Challenge 61–70: Exploring Sets and Dictionaries

In this set of challenges, you'll dive into Python's set and dictionary structures. These exercises cover common operations and methods associated with sets and dictionaries, such as union and intersection for sets, and accessing, updating, and manipulating keys and values for dictionaries.

Challenge 61: Union of Two Sets

Objective: Write a function that takes two sets and returns a new set that is the union of both sets.

```python
# Example Input
set_a = {1, 2, 3}
set_b = {3, 4, 5}

# Expected Output
# {1, 2, 3, 4, 5}
```

Hint: Use the union() method or the | operator to combine elements from both sets without duplicates.

Challenge 62: Intersection of Two Sets

Objective: Write a function that takes two sets and returns a new set containing elements found in both sets.

```python
# Example Input
set_a = {1, 2, 3, 4}
set_b = {3, 4, 5, 6}

# Expected Output
# {3, 4}
```

Hint: Use the intersection() method or the & operator for elements common to both sets.

Challenge 63: Difference Between Two Sets

Objective: Write a function that takes two sets and returns a new set with elements that are in the first set but not in the second.

```python
# Example Input
set_a = {1, 2, 3, 4}
set_b = {3, 4, 5, 6}

# Expected Output
# {1, 2}
```

Hint: Use the difference() method or the - operator.

Challenge 64: Check if a Set is a Subset

Objective: Write a function that takes two sets and checks if the first set is a subset of the second.

```python
# Example Input
set_a = {1, 2}
set_b = {1, 2, 3, 4}

# Expected Output
# True
```

Hint: Use the issubset() method to determine if all elements of the first set are in the second.

Challenge 65: Adding and Removing Elements in a Set

Objective: Write a function that takes a set and an element to add to the set. Then, remove a specified element from the set.

```python
# Example Input
my_set = {1, 2, 3}
to_add = 4
to_remove = 2
```

```
# Expected Output
# {1, 3, 4}
```

Hint: Use the add() and remove() methods for modifying the set.

Challenge 66: Retrieve Dictionary Keys

Objective: Given a dictionary of student names and grades, write a function that returns a list of all student names (keys).

```python
# Example Input
grades = {'Alice': 85, 'Bob': 90, 'Charlie': 78}

# Expected Output
# ['Alice', 'Bob', 'Charlie']
```

Hint: Use the keys() method to obtain all keys from the dictionary.

Challenge 67: Retrieve Dictionary Values

Objective: Write a function that takes a dictionary and returns a list of all values.

```python
# Example Input
grades = {'Alice': 85, 'Bob': 90, 'Charlie': 78}

# Expected Output
# [85, 90, 78]
```

Hint: Use the values() method to collect all values in the dictionary.

Challenge 68: Update a Dictionary Value

Objective: Given a dictionary of student names and grades, write a function that updates the grade of a specified student.

```python
# Example Input
grades = {'Alice': 85, 'Bob': 90, 'Charlie': 78}
student = 'Bob'
new_grade = 95

# Expected Output
# {'Alice': 85, 'Bob': 95, 'Charlie': 78}
```

Hint: Access the dictionary by key to assign the new grade value.

Challenge 69: Check if a Key Exists in a Dictionary

Objective: Write a function that checks if a given key exists in a dictionary.

```python
# Example Input
grades = {'Alice': 85, 'Bob': 90, 'Charlie': 78}
key_to_check = 'Charlie'

# Expected Output
# True
```

Hint: Use the in keyword to test for the presence of a key in the dictionary.

Challenge 70: Dictionary Comprehension

Objective: Use dictionary comprehension to create a new dictionary that maps numbers from 1 to 5 to their squares.

```python
# Expected Output
# {1: 1, 2: 4, 3: 9, 4: 16, 5: 25}
```

Hint: Use a comprehension in the form {key: value for key in iterable}.

These challenges cover essential set operations (union, intersection, difference) and dictionary manipulations, including retrieval and modification of keys and values. Mastering these will enhance your ability to handle complex data in Python with ease.

Solutions and Explanations

This section provides detailed solutions and explanations for each challenge, reinforcing your understanding of set and dictionary operations. Let's walk through each one, focusing on efficient and idiomatic Python solutions.

Challenge 61 Solution: Union of Two Sets

python

```
def union_sets(set_a, set_b):
    return set_a | set_b  # Alternatively, set_a.union(set_b)
```

Explanation: The union operator | or union() method combines elements from both sets, removing duplicates automatically.

Challenge 62 Solution: Intersection of Two Sets

python

```
def intersection_sets(set_a, set_b):
    return set_a & set_b  # Alternatively,
    set_a.intersection(set_b)
```

Explanation: The intersection operator & or intersection() method returns elements common to both sets, creating a new set with those shared values.

Challenge 63 Solution: Difference Between Two Sets

python

```
def difference_sets(set_a, set_b):
    return set_a - set_b  # Alternatively,
    set_a.difference(set_b)
```

Explanation: The difference operator - or difference() method gives elements found in set_a but not in set_b, which can be useful for filtering unique items.

Challenge 64 Solution: Check if a Set is a Subset

python

```
def is_subset(set_a, set_b):
    return set_a.issubset(set_b)
```

Explanation: The issubset() method checks if all elements in set_a are contained within set_b, returning True or False.

Challenge 65 Solution: Adding and Removing Elements in a Set

python

```
def modify_set(my_set, to_add, to_remove):
    my_set.add(to_add)
    my_set.discard(to_remove)  # Discard prevents KeyError if element is absent
    return my_set
```

Explanation: The add() method adds an element to a set. discard() removes an element if it exists, without raising an error if it's not found.

Challenge 66 Solution: Retrieve Dictionary Keys

python

```
def get_keys(grades):
    return list(grades.keys())
```

Explanation: keys() retrieves all dictionary keys. Wrapping it in list() returns them as a list, which can be convenient for iteration or display.

Challenge 67 Solution: Retrieve Dictionary Values

```python
def get_values(grades):
    return list(grades.values())
```

Explanation: Similar to keys(), the values() method fetches all dictionary values, providing insight into the stored data without needing to specify each key.

Challenge 68 Solution: Update a Dictionary Value

```python
def update_grade(grades, student, new_grade):
    grades[student] = new_grade
    return grades
```

Explanation: Assigning a value to an existing key (grades[student] = new_grade) updates that key's value. If the key doesn't exist, this creates it, but you can add a check for existence if needed.

Challenge 69 Solution: Check if a Key Exists in a Dictionary

```python
def key_exists(grades, key_to_check):
    return key_to_check in grades
```

Explanation: The in keyword checks if a key is present in the dictionary, returning a boolean result. This is faster and simpler than fetching values directly.

Challenge 70 Solution: Dictionary Comprehension

```python
def square_numbers():
    return {num: num ** 2 for num in range(1, 6)}
```

Explanation: This dictionary comprehension iterates through numbers 1 to 5, squaring each and storing it as a key-value pair. {num: num ** 2 for num in range(1, 6)} represents a compact and readable way to populate a dictionary based on logic.

These solutions provide effective approaches to handling common operations with sets and dictionaries, demonstrating efficient Python techniques and core methods.

Mini Project 3: "Simple To-Do List with Dictionary"

In this mini-project, you'll create a basic command-line to-do list application using Python dictionaries. This application will allow users to add tasks, mark them as completed, view all tasks, and remove completed tasks. This project will reinforce your understanding of dictionary operations and provide a practical way to manage tasks programmatically.

Project Objective

To build a to-do list manager where tasks can be added, tracked, and removed using a dictionary. The keys will represent task names, and the values will indicate whether a task is completed (True for completed, False for pending).

Step-by-Step Guide

1. Setting Up the To-Do List Dictionary

Start by initializing an empty dictionary to store the tasks. Each task will be stored as a key (task name), with its completion status (True or False) as the value.

```python
todo_list = {}
```

2. Adding a Task

Define a function to add tasks to the to-do list. The function should prompt the user to enter a task name, then add this task to todo_list with a default status of False (not completed).

```python
def add_task(todo_list, task_name):
    todo_list[task_name] = False
    print(f"Task '{task_name}' added.")
```

Example Usage:

```python
add_task(todo_list, "Buy groceries")
add_task(todo_list, "Read Python book")
```

3. Viewing All Tasks

Define a function to display all tasks in the to-do list, indicating whether each task is completed or pending. This will give users an overview of their progress.

```python
def view_tasks(todo_list):
    if not todo_list:
        print("No tasks available.")
        return

    for task, completed in todo_list.items():
        status = "Completed" if completed else "Pending"
        print(f"{task}: {status}")
```

Example Usage:

```python
view_tasks(todo_list)
```

4. Marking a Task as Completed

Define a function that takes a task name as input, searches for it in the dictionary, and updates its status to True (completed). If the task doesn't exist, notify the user.

python

```
def complete_task(todo_list, task_name):
    if task_name in todo_list:
        todo_list[task_name] = True
        print(f"Task '{task_name}' marked as completed.")
    else:
        print(f"Task '{task_name}' not found.")
```

Example Usage:

python

```
complete_task(todo_list, "Buy groceries")
```

5. Removing Completed Tasks

Define a function that removes all tasks marked as completed from the dictionary. This function will iterate through the dictionary and delete any tasks with a status of True.

python

```
def remove_completed_tasks(todo_list):
    completed_tasks = [task for task, completed in
    todo_list.items() if completed]

    for task in completed_tasks:
        del todo_list[task]

    print("All completed tasks removed.")
```

Example Usage:

```python
remove_completed_tasks(todo_list)
```

6. Putting It All Together

Finally, you can create a main function that provides a simple command-line interface, allowing users to choose actions like adding tasks, viewing tasks, marking them as completed, and removing completed tasks.

```python
def main():
    todo_list = {}

    while True:
        print("\nTo-Do List Options:")
        print("1. Add a task")
        print("2. View tasks")
        print("3. Mark task as completed")
        print("4. Remove completed tasks")
        print("5. Exit")

        choice = input("Choose an option (1-5): ")

        if choice == "1":
            task_name = input("Enter task name: ")
            add_task(todo_list, task_name)
        elif choice == "2":
            view_tasks(todo_list)
        elif choice == "3":
            task_name = input("Enter task name to mark as completed: ")
            complete_task(todo_list, task_name)
        elif choice == "4":
            remove_completed_tasks(todo_list)
        elif choice == "5":
            print("Exiting To-Do List.")
```

```
            break
    else:
        print("Invalid option. Please choose between 1 and
        5.")
```

Example Run

```plaintext

To-Do List Options:
1. Add a task
2. View tasks
3. Mark task as completed
4. Remove completed tasks
5. Exit
Choose an option (1-5): 1
Enter task name: Buy groceries
Task 'Buy groceries' added.

Choose an option (1-5): 2
Buy groceries: Pending

Choose an option (1-5): 3
Enter task name to mark as completed: Buy groceries
Task 'Buy groceries' marked as completed.

Choose an option (1-5): 2
Buy groceries: Completed

Choose an option (1-5): 4
All completed tasks removed.

Choose an option (1-5): 2
No tasks available.
```

This project covers key dictionary operations, like adding, updating, and deleting key-value pairs, and provides a useful framework for organizing tasks. Through this mini-project, you'll have hands-on experience with dictionaries and basic control flow in Python, enhancing your problem-solving skills.

Test Your Knowledge: Quiz on Data Structures

Test your understanding of Python's core data structures—lists, tuples, sets, and dictionaries. These questions will help you review key concepts and ensure you're comfortable with choosing and manipulating the right data structures for different tasks.

Quiz Questions

1. What is the main difference between a list and a tuple?
A. Lists are mutable, while tuples are immutable.
B. Tuples are faster for element access.
C. Lists can contain duplicate elements, but tuples cannot.
D. Tuples cannot contain more than five elements.
Answer:

2. Which of the following methods can be used to add an item to a set?
A. .append()
B. .insert()
C. .add()
D. .extend()
Answer:

3. If you want a collection that ensures all elements are unique, which data structure should you use?
A. List
B. Tuple

C. Dictionary
D. Set
Answer:

4. Given a dictionary fruit_colors = {'apple': 'red', 'banana': 'yellow', 'grape': 'purple'}, which code snippet would access the color of 'banana'?
   A. fruit_colors.get('yellow')
   B. fruit_colors['banana']
   C. fruit_colors['yellow']
   D. fruit_colors.get('banana', 'Not found')
Answer:

5. Which of the following can be used to create a shallow copy of a list named my_list?
   A. my_list.copy()
   B. my_list[:]
   C. list(my_list)
   D. All of the above
Answer:

6. What would the following code output?

```python
my_set = {1, 2, 3}
my_set.add(2)
print(my_set)
```

A. {1, 2, 3, 2}
   B. {1, 2, 3}
   C. Error
   D. {1, 2, 3, 4}
Answer:

7. **What is the result of the following code snippet?**

```python
my_tuple = (1, 2, 3)
my_tuple[0] = 10
```

A. (10, 2, 3)
B. Error
C. [10, 2, 3]
D. (1, 10, 3)
Answer:

8. **Which method can be used to safely remove a key-value pair from a dictionary without causing an error if the key doesn't exist?**
A. .pop(key)
B. .discard(key)
C. .popitem()
D. .pop(key, None)
Answer:

9. **What will the following code output?**

```python
numbers = [1, 2, 3]
print(numbers * 2)
```

A. [1, 2, 3, 1, 2, 3]
B. [2, 4, 6]
C. [1, 2, 3, 3, 2, 1]
D. [6]
Answer:

10. **How would you check if the value 'red' is associated with any**

key in the dictionary colors = {'apple': 'red', 'banana': 'yellow', 'grape': 'purple'}?
   A. 'red' in colors
   B. colors.get('red')
   C. 'red' in colors.values()
   D. colors.keys().contains('red')
   Answer:

Answers Key

1. **A** – Lists are mutable, while tuples are immutable.
2. **C** – .add() is the correct method for adding items to a set.
3. **D** – Sets are used for collections with unique items.
4. **B** – fruit_colors['banana'] accesses the color 'yellow' associated with the key 'banana'.
5. **D** – All options provide a shallow copy of a list.
6. **B** – {1, 2, 3}; sets do not allow duplicate elements, so adding 2 again has no effect.
7. **B** – Error; tuples are immutable, so assignment to an index is not allowed.
8. **D** – .pop(key, None) removes the key if it exists; if not, it returns None, preventing an error.
9. **A** – [1, 2, 3, 1, 2, 3]; multiplying a list by 2 repeats its elements.
10. **C** – 'red' in colors.values() checks if 'red' is one of the dictionary values.

This quiz should solidify your grasp on Python's fundamental data structures and their operations, preparing you for more advanced coding challenges.

String Manipulation and Text Processing

Overview: Understanding and Manipulating Strings

Strings are one of the most frequently used data types in Python, essential for working with textual data, generating formatted output, and developing applications that require user input. In Python, strings are immutable sequences of characters, meaning once created, their contents cannot be modified directly. However, Python provides a rich collection of tools and methods that make it easy to manipulate strings, extract and transform data, and format output.

In this chapter, we'll cover the fundamentals of working with strings, explore common string manipulation techniques, and dive into efficient text processing practices. Whether you're processing user inputs, handling file content, or generating reports, a strong understanding of string manipulation will be essential for tackling a wide variety of programming challenges.

Key Concepts in String Manipulation
Basic String Operations

- **Concatenation**: Combining two or more strings using the + operator.
- **Repetition**: Using the * operator to repeat strings a specified number of times.
- **Indexing**: Accessing specific characters within a string using zero-based indices.
- **Slicing**: Extracting substrings using a range of indices.

String Immutability

- Strings in Python cannot be modified after creation. Any operations that appear to modify a string (such as replacing or transforming characters) actually create a new string.

Escape Characters and Raw Strings

- Escape characters like \n (newline), \t (tab), and \\ (backslash) help control the formatting of strings.
- **Raw Strings**: Using an r prefix (e.g., r"string") tells Python to ignore escape characters within the string, which is helpful when working with paths and regular expressions.

String Formatting

- Python offers multiple ways to format strings for better readability, including f-strings (formatted string literals), .format() method, and the % operator.

Common String Methods

- Python strings come with built-in methods for a variety of operations:
- **Case Manipulation**: .upper(), .lower(), .capitalize(), .title()
- **Trimming and Padding**: .strip(), .lstrip(), .rstrip(), .center(), .ljust(), .rjust()
- **Finding and Replacing**: .find(), .index(), .replace()
- **Splitting and Joining**: .split(), .join()
- These methods help with tasks like standardizing input, searching within strings, and combining multiple strings.

Working with Strings in Python
1. String Concatenation and Repetition

STRING MANIPULATION AND TEXT PROCESSING

Concatenation and repetition are straightforward operations that allow you to build larger strings or repeat sequences of text.

```python
# Concatenation
greeting = "Hello" + ", " + "world!"
print(greeting)   # Output: Hello, world!

# Repetition
repeat_phrase = "Hello! " * 3
print(repeat_phrase)   # Output: Hello! Hello! Hello!
```

2. Indexing and Slicing Strings

Since strings are sequences, you can access individual characters or substrings through indexing and slicing.

```python
text = "Python Programming"

# Indexing
print(text[0])    # Output: 'P'
print(text[-1])   # Output: 'g'

# Slicing
print(text[0:6])   # Output: 'Python'
print(text[7:])    # Output: 'Programming'
print(text[::2])   # Output: 'Pto rgamn'
```

Slicing is especially powerful for extracting specific sections of strings, rearranging characters, or reversing the entire string.

3. String Immutability and Creating New Strings

While strings cannot be modified in place, you can use concatenation, slicing, and string methods to generate new, modified strings.

```python
original = "Hello"
modified = original + " World"
print(modified)   # Output: Hello World
```

4. Escape Characters and Raw Strings

Python provides escape sequences for characters that can't be typed directly. For instance, \n inserts a newline, and \t inserts a tab.

```python
text = "Hello\nWorld"
print(text)
# Output:
# Hello
# World

# Raw String
path = r"C:\new_folder\test"
 # Avoids treating backslashes as escape characters
print(path)   # Output: C:\new_folder\test
```

Raw strings are particularly useful when working with regular expressions and file paths on Windows.

String Formatting Techniques
1. f-Strings (Formatted String Literals)

Introduced in Python 3.6, f-strings offer a concise and readable way to embed expressions inside strings.

```python
name = "Alice"
age = 25
```

```
print(f"My name is {name} and I am {age} years old.")
# Output: My name is Alice and I am 25 years old.
```

2. .format() Method

The .format() method is versatile and works across all Python versions.

python

```
template = "Hello, {}. Welcome to {}!"
message = template.format("Alice", "Python Programming")
print(message)
# Output: Hello, Alice. Welcome to Python Programming!
```

3. % Formatting

While older, % formatting can still be used for simple templates.

python

```
name = "Alice"
print("Hello, %s!" % name)   # Output: Hello, Alice!
```

Essential String Methods

1. Case Manipulation

Python provides methods to standardize or adjust the case of strings:

python

```
text = "python programming"
print(text.upper())   # Output: PYTHON PROGRAMMING
print(text.title())   # Output: Python Programming
```

2. Trimming and Padding

Use trimming methods to remove unwanted whitespace or specific characters, and padding methods to align text within a specified width.

```python
text = "   hello   "
print(text.strip())      # Output: 'hello'
print(text.lstrip())     # Output: 'hello   '
print(text.rstrip())     # Output: '   hello'

# Padding
print(text.center(20, '-'))  # Output: '-----   hello   -----'
```

3. Finding and Replacing Substrings

Locate and replace text within strings with .find(), .index(), and .replace().

```python
text = "I love programming in Python"
print(text.find("programming"))   # Output: 7
print(text.replace("Python", "Java"))
  # Output: I love programming in Java
```

4. Splitting and Joining

The .split() method is useful for breaking a string into a list of words or substrings, while .join() concatenates elements into a single string.

```python
text = "Python is fun"
words = text.split()   # Output: ['Python', 'is', 'fun']

# Joining
new_text = ", ".join(words)
print(new_text)  # Output: Python, is, fun
```

Advanced String Processing Techniques

1. Regular Expressions

Python's re module allows for powerful pattern matching within strings. Regular expressions (regex) are especially useful for tasks like validating inputs, searching for patterns, and extracting data.

```python
import re

text = "My phone number is 123-456-7890."
pattern = r"\d{3}-\d{3}-\d{4}"
match = re.search(pattern, text)

if match:
    print("Phone number found:", match.group())
# Output: Phone number found: 123-456-7890
```

2. Handling Multiline Strings

Multiline strings can be handled using triple quotes, which is useful for creating formatted output or including line breaks in text data.

```python
multiline_text = """Hello,
This is a multiline
string in Python."""
print(multiline_text)
```

3. Encoding and Decoding Strings

For working with non-ASCII text, encoding and decoding are essential, particularly for reading from and writing to files with different character sets.

```python
text = "Hello, world!"
encoded_text = text.encode("utf-8")
```

```
print(encoded_text)   # Output: b'Hello, world!'
decoded_text = encoded_text.decode("utf-8")
print(decoded_text)   # Output: Hello, world!
```

This overview provides the foundation needed to approach more advanced topics in text processing, such as tokenization, pattern matching, and text normalization. Understanding and effectively using these tools is key to working with textual data in Python.

Challenge 71–80: Basic String Operations

In these challenges, you'll work on various aspects of string manipulation including indexing, slicing, case changes, and using string methods. These exercises will help you get comfortable with essential string operations, which are crucial for handling and processing text data in Python. The goal is to solidify your understanding of how strings can be accessed, modified, and manipulated effectively.

Challenge 71: Indexing a String

Task:

Given the string text = "Python Programming", retrieve the first character of the string and print it.

Hint:

Use the index 0 to access the first character in the string.

Challenge 72: Negative Indexing

Task:

Given the string text = "Python Programming", retrieve the last character of the string using negative indexing.

Hint:

Use -1 to access the last character.

Challenge 73: String Slicing (Basic)

Task:

Given the string text = "Python Programming", print the substring starting from index 7 and ending at index 16 (not including index 16).

Hint:

Use slicing syntax text[start:end].

Challenge 74: Slicing with Step

Task:

Given the string text = "Python Programming", print every other character in the string.

Hint:

Use the slicing syntax text[start:end:step] with a step value of 2.

Challenge 75: Changing Case (Uppercase)

Task:

Given the string text = "python programming", convert the string to uppercase and print it.

Hint:

Use the .upper() method to convert the string to uppercase.

Challenge 76: Changing Case (Lowercase)

Task:

Given the string text = "PYTHON PROGRAMMING", convert the string to lowercase and print it.

Hint:

Use the .lower() method to convert the string to lowercase.

Challenge 77: Title Case

Task:

Given the string text = "python programming is fun", convert the string to title case (first letter of each word capitalized) and print it.

Hint:

Use the .title() method to convert the string to title case.

Challenge 78: Stripping Whitespace

Task:

Given the string text = " Hello, World! ", remove the leading and trailing whitespace and print the result.

Hint:

Use the .strip() method to remove whitespace from both ends of the string.

Challenge 79: Replacing Substrings

Task:

Given the string text = "I love Python", replace the word "love" with "enjoy" and print the result.

Hint:

Use the .replace() method to replace a substring within the string.

Challenge 80: Checking Substring Existence

Task:

Given the string text = "Python Programming", check if the word "Python" exists in the string and print True or False.

Hint:

Use the in operator to check if a substring exists in a string.

Solutions and Explanations

Solution 71: Indexing a String

```python
text = "Python Programming"
print(text[0])  # Output: P
```

Explanation: In Python, string indexing starts at 0. So text[0] accesses the first character of the string, which is 'P'.

Solution 72: Negative Indexing

```python
text = "Python Programming"
print(text[-1])  # Output: g
```

Explanation: Negative indexing allows access from the end of the string. text[-1] accesses the last character 'g'.

Solution 73: String Slicing (Basic)

STRING MANIPULATION AND TEXT PROCESSING

```python
text = "Python Programming"
print(text[7:16])   # Output: Programming
```

Explanation: Slicing allows you to extract a substring from a string. text[7:16] retrieves characters from index 7 to 15.

Solution 74: Slicing with Step

```python
text = "Python Programming"
print(text[::2])   # Output: Pto rgamn
```

Explanation: The slice text[::2] selects every second character from the string, resulting in 'Pto rgamn'.

Solution 75: Changing Case (Uppercase)

```python
text = "python programming"
print(text.upper())   # Output: PYTHON PROGRAMMING
```

Explanation: The .upper() method converts all characters in the string to uppercase.

Solution 76: Changing Case (Lowercase)

```python
text = "PYTHON PROGRAMMING"
print(text.lower())   # Output: python programming
```

Explanation: The .lower() method converts all characters in the string to lowercase.

Solution 77: Title Case

```python
text = "python programming is fun"
print(text.title())   # Output: Python Programming Is Fun
```

Explanation: The .title() method capitalizes the first letter of each word in the string.

Solution 78: Stripping Whitespace

```python
text = "   Hello, World!   "
print(text.strip())   # Output: Hello, World!
```

Explanation: The .strip() method removes any leading or trailing whitespace from the string.

Solution 79: Replacing Substrings

```python
text = "I love Python"
print(text.replace("love", "enjoy"))   # Output: I enjoy Python
```

Explanation: The .replace() method replaces occurrences of a specified substring with another.

Solution 80: Checking Substring Existence

```python
text = "Python Programming"
print("Python" in text)   # Output: True
```

Explanation: The in operator checks if the substring "Python" is present in the string text.

These challenges have introduced you to the essential string operations you'll often encounter when manipulating text in Python. By mastering these techniques, you'll be well-equipped to handle a wide variety of tasks, from formatting output to parsing data in real-world applications.

Challenge 81–90: Advanced String Challenges

In these challenges, we will explore more advanced aspects of string manipulation, focusing on regular expressions (regex), pattern matching, and input validation. Regular expressions are powerful tools that allow you to search for and manipulate strings based on specific patterns, which is useful for tasks like validating user inputs, processing text, and working with complex string structures. These challenges will help you gain a deeper understanding of regular expressions and apply them in real-world scenarios.

Challenge 81: Basic Pattern Matching with re.search()

Task:

Use the re.search() function to check if the string "Python 3" contains the number "3".

Hint:

Use the regular expression pattern r"\d" to match a digit.

Challenge 82: Matching Specific Words

Task:

Given the string text = "Python is easy and fun", use a regular expression to find the word "easy" in the string.

Hint:

Use re.search(r"\beasy\b", text) to match the word exactly.

Challenge 83: Matching Multiple Words

Task:

Given the string text = "Python is fun and Python is easy", write a regular expression to find all occurrences of the word "Python" in the string.

Hint:

Use the regular expression pattern r"\bPython\b" to match the word "Python", and use re.findall() to retrieve all occurrences.

Challenge 84: Validating Email Addresses

Task:

Write a regular expression to validate if the input string is a valid email address. The format should be username@domain.com, where the username can contain letters, digits, and underscores, and the domain can contain letters and dots.

Hint:

Use the following regular expression pattern:

r"^[a-zA-Z0-9_]+@[a-zA-Z]+\.[a-zA-Z]{2,}$"

Challenge 85: Extracting Numbers from a String

Task:

Given the string text = "The price is 100 dollars and 50 cents", write a regular expression to extract the numbers (100 and 50) from the string.

Hint:

Use the regular expression pattern r"\d+" to find all digits in the string.

Challenge 86: Matching Phone Numbers

Task:

Given a string text = "Call us at 123-456-7890 or 987-654-3210", write a regular expression to extract both phone numbers.

Hint:

Use the regular expression pattern r"\d{3}-\d{3}-\d{4}" to match phone numbers in the format xxx-xxx-xxxx.

Challenge 87: Password Validation

Task:

Write a regular expression to validate a password. The password must be at least 8 characters long, contain at least one uppercase letter, one lowercase letter, one digit, and one special character (e.g., @, #, $, %).

Hint:

Use the following regular expression pattern:

r"^(?=.*[a-z])(?=.*[A-Z])(?=.*\d)(?=.*[!@#$%^&*])[A-Za-z\d!@#$%^&*]{8,}$"

Challenge 88: Finding Date Formats

Task:

Write a regular expression to match dates in the format DD-MM-YYYY (e.g., 01-12-2024).

STRING MANIPULATION AND TEXT PROCESSING

Hint:

Use the regular expression pattern r"\d{2}-\d{2}-\d{4}" to match the date format.

Challenge 89: Removing Extra Whitespace

Task:

Given the string text = " Python is fun ", remove all leading, trailing, and extra spaces between words using a regular expression.

Hint:

Use the regular expression pattern r"\s+" to match one or more spaces, and replace it with a single space.

Challenge 90: Matching and Replacing Text

Task:

Given the string text = "Hello, World! Welcome to Python programming.", write a regular expression to replace the word "Python" with "Java".

Hint:

Use the re.sub() function with the regular expression pattern r"\bPython\b" to match the word "Python" and replace it.

Solutions and Explanations

Solution 81: Basic Pattern Matching with re.search()

```python
import re

text = "Python 3"
match = re.search(r"\d", text)
if match:
    print("Digit found!")   # Output: Digit found!
else:
    print("No digit found.")
```

Explanation: The regular expression r"\d" matches any digit in the string. The re.search() function checks if this pattern exists in the string, and if it does, prints "Digit found!".

Solution 82: Matching Specific Words

python

```
import re

text = "Python is easy and fun"
match = re.search(r"\beasy\b", text)
if match:
    print("Word 'easy' found!")  # Output: Word 'easy' found!
else:
    print("Word 'easy' not found.")
```

Explanation: The regular expression r"\beasy\b" ensures that the word "easy" is matched exactly, without being part of another word.

Solution 83: Matching Multiple Words

python

```
import re

text = "Python is fun and Python is easy"
matches = re.findall(r"\bPython\b", text)
print(matches)  # Output: ['Python', 'Python']
```

Explanation: The re.findall() function finds all occurrences of the word "Python", using the pattern r"\bPython\b", which ensures it matches the word exactly.

Solution 84: Validating Email Addresses

python

```
import re

email = "user@example.com"
match = re.match(r"^[a-zA-Z0-9_
```

```
]+@[a-zA-Z]+\.
[a-zA-Z]{2,}
$", email)
if match:
    print("Valid email address!")   # Output: Valid email address!
else:
    print("Invalid email address.")
```

Explanation: The regular expression r"^[a-zA-Z0-9_]+@[a-zA-Z]+\.[a-zA-Z]{2,}$" matches valid email addresses by ensuring the correct structure (username, @, domain, .com).

Solution 85: Extracting Numbers from a String

python

```
import re

text = "The price is 100 dollars and 50 cents"
numbers = re.findall(r"\d+", text)
print(numbers)   # Output: ['100', '50']
```

Explanation: The regular expression r"\d+" finds all sequences of digits in the string, which are then returned as a list.

Solution 86: Matching Phone Numbers

python

```
import re

text = "Call us at 123-456-7890 or 987-654-3210"
phone_numbers = re.findall(r"\d{3}-\d{3}-\d{4}", text)
print(phone_numbers)   # Output: ['123-456-7890', '987-654-3210']
```

Explanation: The regular expression r"\d{3}-\d{3}-\d{4}" matches phone numbers in the format xxx-xxx-xxxx.

Solution 87: Password Validation

```python
import re

password = "Python@123"
match = re.match(r"^(?=.*[a-z])
(?=.*[A-Z])
(?=.*\d)
(?=.*[!@#$%^&*])
[A-Za-z\d!@#$%^&*]
{8,}$", password)
if match:
    print("Valid password!")  # Output: Valid password!
else:
    print("Invalid password.")
```

Explanation: The regular expression ensures the password has at least one lowercase letter, one uppercase letter, one digit, and one special character, and is at least 8 characters long.

Solution 88: Finding Date Formats

```python
import re

text = "Today's date is 01-12-2024"
match = re.search(r"\d{2}-\d{2}-\d{4}", text)
if match:
    print(f"Found date: {match.group()}")
# Output: Found date: 01-12-2024
```

Explanation: The regular expression r"\d{2}-\d{2}-\d{4}" matches the date format DD-MM-YYYY.

Solution 89: Removing Extra Whitespace

```python
import re

text = "   Python    is    fun   "
clean_text = re.sub(r"\s+", " ", text.strip())
print(clean_text)  # Output: Python is fun
```

Explanation: The re.sub(r"\s+", " ", text.strip()) removes extra whitespace between words and trims leading/trailing spaces.

Solution 90: Matching and Replacing Text

```python
import re

text = "Hello, World! Welcome to Python programming."
new_text = re.sub(r"\bPython\b", "Java", text)
print(new_text)  # Output: Hello, World!
Welcome to Java programming.
```

Explanation: The re.sub() function replaces the word "Python" with "Java" using the regular expression pattern r"\bPython\b", which matches the exact word.

These challenges have introduced you to the power of regular expressions in Python. Regular expressions are incredibly versatile and can be used for tasks like searching, replacing, and validating text. By mastering them, you can efficiently tackle more complex text-processing problems.

Solutions and Explanations (Continued)

Let's dive deeper into the solutions and provide detailed explanations for each challenge.

Solution 81: Basic Pattern Matching with re.search()

```python
import re

text = "Python 3"
match = re.search(r"\d", text)
if match:
    print("Digit found!")  # Output: Digit found!
else:
    print("No digit found.")
```

Explanation:

- The regular expression r"\d" is used to match any digit in the string. The re.search() function looks for the first occurrence of this pattern in the provided string.
- Since the string "Python 3" contains the digit 3, re.search() returns a match, and the message "Digit found!" is printed.

Solution 82: Matching Specific Words

```python
import re

text = "Python is easy and fun"
match = re.search(r"\beasy\b", text)
if match:
    print("Word 'easy' found!")  # Output: Word 'easy' found!
else:
    print("Word 'easy' not found.")
```

Explanation:

- \b represents a word boundary, ensuring that the word "easy" is matched exactly and not as part of a larger word (e.g., "easily").

STRING MANIPULATION AND TEXT PROCESSING

- The re.search() function checks if "easy" appears as a separate word within the string. Since it does, the match is successful, and "Word 'easy' found!" is printed.

Solution 83: Matching Multiple Words

```python
import re

text = "Python is fun and Python is easy"
matches = re.findall(r"\bPython\b", text)
print(matches)  # Output: ['Python', 'Python']
```

Explanation:

- The regular expression pattern r"\bPython\b" is used to match the word "Python" wherever it appears, surrounded by word boundaries.
- The re.findall() function finds all occurrences of the word "Python" in the string, returning a list of the matches: ['Python', 'Python'].

Solution 84: Validating Email Addresses

```python
import re

email = "user@example.com"
match = re.match(r"^[a-zA-Z0-9_]+@[a-zA-Z]+\.[a-zA-Z]{2,}$", email)
if match:
    print("Valid email address!")   # Output: Valid email address!
else:
    print("Invalid email address.")
```

Explanation:

- This regular expression r"^[a-zA-Z0-9_]+@[a-zA-Z]+\.[a-zA-Z]{2,}$" is designed to match email addresses. Here's a breakdown:
- ^[a-zA-Z0-9_]+: Matches the start of the string, followed by one or more alphanumeric characters or underscores (valid username characters).
- @: Matches the "@" symbol.
- [a-zA-Z]+: Matches one or more alphabetic characters (valid domain name characters).
- \.: Matches the dot (.) separator.
- [a-zA-Z]{2,}$: Matches the domain extension with at least two letters (e.g., .com, .org).
- If the email matches this pattern, it's considered valid, and the message "Valid email address!" is printed.

Solution 85: Extracting Numbers from a String

python

```
import re

text = "The price is 100 dollars and 50 cents"
numbers = re.findall(r"\d+", text)
print(numbers)  # Output: ['100', '50']
```

Explanation:

- The regular expression r"\d+" matches one or more digits (denoted by \d), and + ensures that it captures groups of digits that are together.
- The re.findall() function returns all occurrences of this pattern in the string. Here, it finds the numbers "100" and "50".

Solution 86: Matching Phone Numbers

STRING MANIPULATION AND TEXT PROCESSING

```python
import re

text = "Call us at 123-456-7890 or 987-654-3210"
phone_numbers = re.findall
(r"\d{3}-\d{3}-\d{4}", text)
print(phone_numbers)  # Output:
 ['123-456-7890', '987-654-3210']
```

Explanation:

- The regular expression pattern r"\d{3}-\d{3}-\d{4}" is designed to match phone numbers in the format xxx-xxx-xxxx, where \d{3} matches exactly three digits, and - matches the hyphen separator.
- re.findall() identifies and returns all phone numbers in this format from the string.

Solution 87: Password Validation

```python
import re

password = "Python@123"
match = re.match(r"^(?=.*
[a-z])(?=.*[A-Z])
(?=.*\d)(?=.
*[!@#$%^&*])[A-Za-z\d
!@#$%^&*]{8,}$", password)
if match:
    print("Valid password!")  # Output: Valid password!
else:
    print("Invalid password.")
```

Explanation:

- This regular expression ensures the password meets the following criteria:
- ^(?=.*[a-z]): At least one lowercase letter.
- (?=.*[A-Z]): At least one uppercase letter.
- (?=.*\d): At least one digit.
- (?=.*[!@#$%^&*]): At least one special character (e.g., @, #, $).
- [A-Za-z\d!@#$%^&*]{8,}$: The password must be at least 8 characters long and consist of valid characters.
- re.match() checks if the password satisfies all these conditions and validates it accordingly.

Solution 88: Finding Date Formats

python

```
import re

text = "Today's date is 01-12-2024"
match = re.search(r"\d{2}-\d{2}-\d{4}", text)
if match:
    print(f"Found date: {match.group()}")
# Output: Found date: 01-12-2024
```

Explanation:

- The regular expression r"\d{2}-\d{2}-\d{4}" is designed to match dates in the format DD-MM-YYYY.
- \d{2} matches exactly two digits for the day and month.
- \d{4} matches four digits for the year.
- - matches the hyphen separator.
- re.search() is used to find the first occurrence of a date in the string.

Solution 89: Removing Extra Whitespace

STRING MANIPULATION AND TEXT PROCESSING

```python
import re

text = "   Python     is    fun   "
clean_text = re.sub(r"\s+", " ", text.strip())
print(clean_text)  # Output: Python is fun
```

Explanation:

- The text.strip() function removes any leading or trailing spaces from the string.
- The re.sub(r"\s+", " ", ...) function replaces all sequences of whitespace characters (one or more spaces, tabs, etc.) with a single space.
- This ensures that extra spaces between words are removed, and only a single space remains between words.

Solution 90: Matching and Replacing Text

```python
import re

text = "Hello, World! Welcome to Python programming."
new_text = re.sub
(r"\bPython\b", "Java", text)
print(new_text)  # Output: Hello,
 World! Welcome to Java programming.
```

Explanation:

- The regular expression r"\bPython\b" matches the word "Python" exactly. The \b ensures it is a whole word and not part of another word.
- The re.sub() function replaces the matched word with "Java", producing the new string "Hello, World! Welcome to Java programming.".

With these advanced string challenges, you've been introduced to powerful concepts like regular expressions, which are crucial for pattern matching, input validation, and advanced string manipulation. Regular expressions are a powerful tool in Python that, when mastered, can greatly enhance your ability to work with and process text data. Whether you're working with form inputs, parsing complex text files, or extracting valuable data, regular expressions will make these tasks more efficient and straightforward.

Mini Project 4: "Password Generator"

In this mini project, we will create a Python program that generates secure passwords. The program will allow users to specify the length of the password and choose whether they want to include special characters, digits, and uppercase letters. We will employ the concepts we've learned in this chapter, such as string manipulation, random number generation, and regular expressions for validation.

Project Overview

The goal of this project is to design a Python program that generates a random password based on the user's requirements. The program will:
1. Allow the user to choose the length of the password.
2. Allow the user to decide whether to include uppercase letters, digits, and special characters.
3. Generate a password that meets the selected criteria.
4. Ensure the generated password is both strong and meets common security requirements.

Step 1: Setting Up the Password Generator

Let's begin by writing the basic structure of the program and asking the user for their preferences.

STRING MANIPULATION AND TEXT PROCESSING

```python
import random
import string

def generate_password(length=8, use_uppercase=True, use_digits=True, use_special=True):
    # Define the character sets
    lowercase = string.ascii_lowercase
    uppercase = string.ascii_uppercase if use_uppercase else ''
    digits = string.digits if use_digits else ''
    special_characters = string.punctuation if use_special else ''

    # Combine all character sets
    all_characters = lowercase + uppercase + digits + special_characters

    # Check if any character set is empty
    if not all_characters:
        raise ValueError("At least one character set must be selected.")

    # Generate a random password by selecting random characters from the combined set
    password = ''.join(random.choice(all_characters) for _ in range(length))

    return password
```

Explanation:
Character Sets:

- We use Python's string module to access predefined sets of characters:
- string.ascii_lowercase for lowercase letters (a-z).
- string.ascii_uppercase for uppercase letters (A-Z).
- string.digits for digits (0-9).
- string.punctuation for special characters (e.g., !@#$%^&*).

- Based on user input, we include the desired character sets by adding them together.

Random Password Generation:

- The random.choice() function randomly selects a character from the combined character set. We repeat this process for the desired password length, generating a string that represents the password.

Error Handling:

- If no character sets are selected (i.e., the user opts for none of the available categories), a ValueError is raised to ensure the program doesn't proceed with an empty set.

Step 2: Enhancing the Program with User Input

Next, we'll enhance the program by prompting the user for input so they can specify their password requirements.

```python
def main():
    # Welcome message
    print("Welcome to the Password Generator!")

    # Get user preferences for the password
    length = int(input("Enter the desired password length: "))
    use_uppercase = input("Include uppercase letters? (yes/no): ").lower() == 'yes'
    use_digits = input("Include digits? (yes/no): ").lower() == 'yes'
    use_special = input("Include special characters? (yes/no): ").lower() == 'yes'

    # Generate the password
```

```
    try:
        password = generate_password(length, use_uppercase,
        use_digits, use_special)
        print(f"Your generated password is: {password}")
    except ValueError as e:
        print(e)

if __name__ == "__main__":
    main()
```

Explanation:
User Input:

- We ask the user to specify the length of the password and whether they want to include uppercase letters, digits, and special characters. The input() function is used to capture these choices.
- The lower() method ensures that the user input is case-insensitive, and we check if the input is 'yes' to decide whether the respective character sets are included.

Generating and Displaying the Password:

- Once the user has specified their preferences, we call the generate_password() function to generate a password based on the input.
- If the user chooses to include all character types (lowercase, uppercase, digits, special characters), the program combines them and generates a secure password.
- The password is printed out for the user to see.

Error Handling:

- If the user selects invalid combinations (for example, no character sets are chosen), the program will raise and display a ValueError, ensuring that the user is prompted to make a valid selection.

Step 3: Adding Validation and Security Features

To ensure the password is truly strong, we can add a validation feature that checks for the presence of at least one character from each selected character set.

python

```
def validate_password(password, use_uppercase, use_digits, use_special):
    if use_uppercase and not any(char.isupper() for char in password):
        return False
    if use_digits and not any(char.isdigit() for char in password):
        return False
    if use_special and not any(char in string.punctuation for char in password):
        return False
    return True
```

Explanation:

- **Validation Logic:**
- After generating the password, the validate_password() function checks whether the generated password contains at least one character from each of the selected sets:
- If the user has requested uppercase letters, the password must contain at least one uppercase letter.
- Similarly, if digits and special characters are requested, the password must contain at least one of each.
- The function returns True if the password meets the criteria; otherwise, it returns False.

Step 4: Integrating Validation into the Main Program

We can now integrate this validation into the main program, ensuring that the password meets all the required conditions before presenting it to the user.

```python
def main():
    print("Welcome to the Password Generator!")

    length = int(input("Enter the desired password length: "))
    use_uppercase = input("Include uppercase letters? (yes/no): ").lower() == 'yes'
    use_digits = input("Include digits? (yes/no): ").lower() == 'yes'
    use_special = input("Include special characters? (yes/no): ").lower() == 'yes'

    try:
        password = generate_password(length, use_uppercase, use_digits, use_special)

        if validate_password(password, use_uppercase, use_digits, use_special):
            print(f"Your generated password is: {password}")
        else:
            print("The generated password does not meet the specified criteria. Regenerating...")
            password = generate_password(length, use_uppercase, use_digits, use_special)
            print(f"New password: {password}")

    except ValueError as e:
        print(e)

if __name__ == "__main__":
    main()
```

Explanation:

- **Password Validation:**
- After generating the password, we call validate_password() to ensure the password matches the user's specifications.

- If the password is valid, it is displayed; otherwise, a new password is generated.

In this mini project, we created a Python program that allows the user to generate secure passwords based on customizable criteria. By utilizing the random and string modules, we were able to generate a password of the specified length and include various character types based on user input. Additionally, we added a password validation feature to ensure that the generated password meets all the required conditions. This project is a great way to apply string manipulation and randomization skills while reinforcing the importance of password security.

Test Your Knowledge: Quiz on Strings and Text Processing

This quick quiz will help you review and solidify the concepts covered in this chapter on string manipulation and text processing. Answer the following questions to test your understanding of string operations, regular expressions, and text handling in Python.

1. **String Indexing**

   What will the following code print?

   ```python
   s = "Python Programming"
   print(s[7:10])
   ```

   A) "Pro"
   B) "Pyt"
   C) "og"
   D) "Progr"

2. **String Methods**

Which of the following methods is used to convert a string to all uppercase letters?
A) str.upper()
B) str.lower()
C) str.capitalize()
D) str.swapcase()

3. String Slicing
Given the string text = "Hello World!", what will text[6:] return?
A) "Hello "
B) "World!"
C) "Hello World!"
D) " "

4. Regular Expressions
Which Python module do you need to import to work with regular expressions?
A) re
B) regex
C) regexp
D) text

5. String Concatenation
Which of the following statements correctly concatenates the strings word1 and word2?
A) word1 + word2
B) word1 - word2
C) word1 . word2
D) word1 * word2

6. String Search
What is the output of the following code?

```python
s = "The quick brown fox jumps over the lazy dog"
print(s.find("fox"))
```

A) 0

B) 1

C) 16

D) -1

7. **Escape Sequences**

Which of the following escape sequences represents a new line in a string?

A) \\n

B) \n

C) \r

D) \t

8. **String Methods**

What is the output of the following code?

```python
s = "   Hello, World!   "
print(s.strip())
```

A) "Hello, World!"

B) "Hello World!"

C) " Hello, World! "

D) "World!"

9. **String Formatting**

Which string formatting method is used in the following code?

STRING MANIPULATION AND TEXT PROCESSING

```python
name = "John"
age = 30
print(f"My name is {name} and I am {age} years old.")
```

A) .format()
B) % operator
C) f-string (formatted string literal)
D) str.format()

10. **Regular Expressions**

Which regular expression pattern will match a string that contains only digits?

A) \d+
B) \w+
C) [A-Za-z]
D) \D+

Answer Key:

1. **A)** "Pro"
2. **A)** str.upper()
3. **B)** "World!"
4. **A)** re
5. **A)** word1 + word2
6. **C)** 16
7. **B)** \n
8. **A)** "Hello, World!"
9. **C)** f-string (formatted string literal)
10. **A)** \d+

This quiz will help reinforce your understanding of how to manipulate strings, apply regular expressions, and use string methods in Python. Make sure you go back to any topics you're unsure about to strengthen your grasp of string operations in Python.

Working with Files and Basic Data Handling

Overview: Reading from and Writing to Files

In this chapter, we will dive into one of the most essential skills in programming: reading from and writing to files. Files are a central part of most applications and are crucial for data persistence. Whether it's saving user input, logging application events, or processing large datasets, knowing how to effectively handle files is key for developing robust applications.

Python provides built-in functions and libraries to make file handling easy and efficient. In this section, we will cover how to:

1. Open and close files.
2. Read content from files.
3. Write content to files.
4. Handle different file modes.
5. Work with both text and binary files.
6. Manage file exceptions and errors effectively.

By the end of this chapter, you will understand the fundamental concepts and techniques necessary for reading from and writing to files in Python, as well as how to apply them in real-world scenarios.

1. Opening and Closing Files

To work with files, you first need to open them using the open() function. This function allows you to specify the file's path and the mode in which you want to open the file.

The basic syntax for opening a file is:

```python
file = open('filename', 'mode')
```

The mode parameter defines the type of operations you can perform on the file. Common file modes include:

- 'r': Read (default mode). Opens the file for reading. The file must exist.
- 'w': Write. Opens the file for writing. If the file exists, it will be overwritten; if it doesn't, a new file will be created.
- 'a': Append. Opens the file for appending. If the file exists, the new content will be added at the end.
- 'rb': Read in binary mode. Opens the file for reading in binary format.
- 'wb': Write in binary mode. Opens the file for writing in binary format.

Once you're done working with a file, it's important to close it using the close() method:

```python
file.close()
```

This ensures that all resources are properly released and that any changes made to the file are saved.

Example of Opening and Closing a File:

```python
file = open('example.txt', 'w')
file.write("Hello, Python World!")
file.close()
```

2. Reading from Files

Reading from files is a fundamental operation when working with file I/O. Python provides multiple methods to read content from a file. These methods can be categorized as follows:

- read(): Reads the entire file at once and returns it as a string.
- readline(): Reads a single line from the file.
- readlines(): Reads all the lines in a file and returns them as a list of strings.

Example: Reading the Entire File

```python
file = open('example.txt', 'r')
content = file.read()   # Read all content in the file
print(content)
file.close()
```

Example: Reading Line by Line

```python
file = open('example.txt', 'r')
line1 = file.readline()   # Read the first line
print(line1)
```

```python
line2 = file.readline()  # Read the second line
print(line2)
file.close()
```

Example: Reading All Lines as a List

```python
file = open('example.txt', 'r')
lines = file.readlines()  # Read all lines as a list
for line in lines:
    print(line.strip())  # Remove extra newline characters
file.close()
```

When using readlines(), each line from the file will be stored as an element in the returned list. You can iterate over this list to process each line individually.

3. Writing to Files

Writing to files is just as important as reading from them. There are various ways to write data to files in Python, depending on whether you want to overwrite, append, or create new files.

- write(): Writes a string to the file. If the file does not exist, it will be created.
- writelines(): Writes a list of strings to the file, with each string on a separate line.

Example: Writing to a New File (Overwriting)

```python
file = open('output.txt', 'w')
file.write("This is a new file.\nWelcome to Python file
```

```
handling.")
file.close()
```

Example: Appending to a File

python

```python
file = open('output.txt', 'a')
file.write("\nAppending a new line to the file.")
file.close()
```

Example: Writing Multiple Lines

python

```python
file = open('output.txt', 'w')
lines = ["First line\n", "Second line\n", "Third line\n"]
file.writelines(lines)
file.close()
```

In this case, we provide a list of strings, and each string will be written on a new line.

4. Working with Text vs. Binary Files

Files can be either text files or binary files. Text files contain readable characters (like .txt or .csv files), while binary files store data in binary format (like images, videos, or executable files).

To read or write binary files, you need to open the file in binary mode by using the 'b' character in the file mode.

Example: Writing Binary Data to a File

python

```python
data = b"Hello, this is binary data."  # A bytes object
file = open('binary_output.bin', 'wb')
```

```
file.write(data)
file.close()
```

Example: Reading Binary Data from a File

```python
file = open('binary_output.bin', 'rb')
binary_data = file.read()
print(binary_data)
file.close()
```

When handling binary files, you will typically work with byte objects (b'...') rather than strings.

5. File Exception Handling

While working with files, it's important to handle potential exceptions that may arise. These include errors like attempting to read from a non-existent file or trying to write to a file that is read-only.

Python's try and except blocks allow you to manage file-related errors gracefully.

Example: Handling File Not Found Error

```python
try:
    file = open('non_existent_file.txt', 'r')
    content = file.read()
    print(content)
except FileNotFoundError:
    print("The file was not found.")
finally:
    file.close()
```

In this example, the FileNotFoundError exception is caught, and an appropriate message is displayed. The finally block ensures that the file is

WORKING WITH FILES AND BASIC DATA HANDLING

closed, even if an error occurs.

6. Context Managers (with Statement)

A best practice when working with files is to use the with statement, which automatically handles opening and closing the file for you, even if an exception is raised. This eliminates the need to explicitly call close() and ensures that resources are properly managed.

Example: Using with to Open and Close Files

```python
with open('example.txt', 'r') as file:
    content = file.read()
    print(content)
```

Here, the file is automatically closed once the block inside the with statement finishes executing, even if an error occurs inside the block.

In this section, we've covered the basics of reading from and writing to files in Python. Understanding how to handle files is a crucial skill in any Python programmer's toolkit, whether you're building an application that saves user data, working with log files, or processing large datasets.

We've explored:
- How to open and close files.
- Various methods for reading and writing files.
- The difference between text and binary files.
- How to handle exceptions that may occur during file operations.
- The benefits of using context managers to simplify file handling.

Mastering file handling and data manipulation opens the door to building more powerful and flexible Python programs.

Challenge 91-100: File Handling Basics

In this section, we will tackle a series of challenges designed to reinforce your understanding of basic file handling in Python. You will work on problems that involve reading from files, writing to files, appending data, and managing file paths. These exercises will help you practice the core concepts introduced in the previous sections and make sure you are comfortable working with files.

Challenge 91: Reading from a File

Task: Write a Python function that reads the contents of a file and prints each line.

```python
def read_file(file_path):
    # Your code here
```

Hint: Use the readlines() method to read all lines in a file.

Challenge 92: Writing to a File

Task: Write a Python function that takes a list of strings and writes each string to a new file. Each string should be written to a new line in the file.

```python
def write_to_file(file_path, lines):
    # Your code here
```

Hint: Use the writelines() method to write multiple lines at once.

Challenge 93: Appending to a File

Task: Write a Python function that appends a new line of text to an existing file.

```python
def append_to_file(file_path, line):
    # Your code here
```

Hint: Use the 'a' mode for appending to the file.

Challenge 94: File Not Found Error

Task: Write a Python function that tries to open a file. If the file does not exist, print a message saying, "File not found." If the file is opened successfully, print its contents.

```python
def open_file(file_path):
    # Your code here
```

Hint: Use a try-except block to catch the FileNotFoundError.

Challenge 95: Read and Count Lines

Task: Write a Python function that reads a file and counts how many lines are in it.

```python
def count_lines(file_path):
    # Your code here
```

Hint: Use the readlines() method to get all lines and then count them.

Challenge 96: File Path Check

Task: Write a Python function that checks if a file exists at a given path. If the file exists, return True; otherwise, return False.

```python
import os

def file_exists(file_path):
    # Your code here
```

Hint: Use the os.path.exists() method to check for file existence.

Challenge 97: Read First N Lines

Task: Write a Python function that reads and prints the first N lines of a file.

```python
def read_first_n_lines(file_path, n):
    # Your code here
```

Hint: Use a for loop to iterate over the first n lines of the file.

Challenge 98: Write Numbers to a File

Task: Write a Python function that writes the numbers from 1 to 100 into a file, one number per line.

```python
def write_numbers_to_file(file_path):
    # Your code here
```

Hint: Use a for loop and the write() method to write numbers.

Challenge 99: Copy File Contents

Task: Write a Python function that copies the contents of one file to another. Ensure that if the destination file does not exist, it is created.

```python
def copy_file(src_file, dest_file):
    # Your code here
```

Hint: Open both the source and destination files in appropriate modes ('r' for reading and 'w' for writing).

Challenge 100: Read and Reverse File Contents

Task: Write a Python function that reads the contents of a file and prints the contents in reverse order (line by line).

```python
def reverse_file_contents(file_path):
    # Your code here
```

Hint: Use the readlines() method to read the file and then reverse the list of lines using slicing.

Solutions and Explanations

Below are solutions and explanations for each of the above challenges to help reinforce the concepts covered.

Solution to Challenge 91: Reading from a File

```python
def read_file(file_path):
    try:
        with open(file_path, 'r') as file:
            for line in file:
                print(line.strip())  # Use strip to remove extra
                newlines
    except FileNotFoundError:
        print("File not found.")
```

Explanation: This function uses the with statement to open the file in read mode. Each line is read and printed using a for loop. The strip() method is used to remove trailing newline characters.

Solution to Challenge 92: Writing to a File

```python
def write_to_file(file_path, lines):
    with open(file_path, 'w') as file:
        file.writelines(lines)
```

Explanation: The function writes each string from the list lines to the file, with each string on a new line. The 'w' mode overwrites any existing file.

Solution to Challenge 93: Appending to a File

```python
def append_to_file(file_path, line):
    with open(file_path, 'a') as file:
        file.write(line + '\n')
```

Explanation: This function opens the file in append mode ('a') and writes the new line at the end of the file.

Solution to Challenge 94: File Not Found Error

```python
def open_file(file_path):
    try:
        with open(file_path, 'r') as file:
            print(file.read())
    except FileNotFoundError:
        print("File not found.")
```

Explanation: A try-except block is used to catch the FileNotFoundError and print an appropriate message if the file doesn't exist.

Solution to Challenge 95: Read and Count Lines

```python
def count_lines(file_path):
    with open(file_path, 'r') as file:
        lines = file.readlines()
        return len(lines)
```

Explanation: The readlines() method is used to get all lines in the file as a list, and the len() function is used to count the number of lines.

Solution to Challenge 96: File Path Check

```python
import os

def file_exists(file_path):
    return os.path.exists(file_path)
```

Explanation: This function uses the os.path.exists() method to check if the file exists at the specified path.

Solution to Challenge 97: Read First N Lines

```python
def read_first_n_lines(file_path, n):
    with open(file_path, 'r') as file:
        for i in range(n):
            print(file.readline().strip())  # Read and print each line
```

Explanation: A for loop is used to read and print the first n lines from the file.

Solution to Challenge 98: Write Numbers to a File

```python
def write_numbers_to_file(file_path):
    with open(file_path, 'w') as file:
        for i in range(1, 101):
            file.write(f"{i}\n")
```

Explanation: A for loop is used to write the numbers from 1 to 100, one per line, into the file.

Solution to Challenge 99: Copy File Contents

```python
def copy_file(src_file, dest_file):
    with open(src_file, 'r') as src:
        with open(dest_file, 'w') as dest:
            dest.write(src.read())
```

Explanation: This function reads the contents of the source file and writes them to the destination file. If the destination file does not exist, it will be created.

Solution to Challenge 100: Read and Reverse File Contents

```python
def reverse_file_contents(file_path):
    with open(file_path, 'r') as file:
        lines = file.readlines()
        for line in reversed(lines):
            print(line.strip())
```

Explanation: The function reads all lines from the file, reverses the list using reversed(), and prints each line in reverse order.

These challenges provide a hands-on approach to mastering basic file handling in Python, including reading, writing, appending, and managing file paths. By completing these exercises, you'll gain confidence in working with files and data manipulation, which are fundamental skills for many Python applications.

Challenge 101–110: Processing Data from Files

In this section, you will dive deeper into processing data from files, specifically focusing on text processing, basic data analysis, and handling CSV files. These challenges will help you develop the necessary skills to work with real-world data, from cleaning and analyzing data to extracting information from structured file formats.

Challenge 101: Counting Word Frequency in a Text File

Task: Write a Python function that reads a text file and counts how many times each word appears. The function should return a dictionary where the keys are words and the values are the number of occurrences.

```python
def count_word_frequency(file_path):
    # Your code here
```

Hint: Use the split() method to break the text into words and the collections.Counter class to count occurrences.

Challenge 102: Extracting Specific Data from a File

Task: Write a Python function that reads a file containing names and ages (one per line in the format Name: Age). The function should return a list of tuples where each tuple contains a name and an age (as an integer).

Example input:

```makefile
John: 25
Alice: 30
Bob: 22
```

```python
def extract_name_age(file_path):
    # Your code here
```

Hint: Use string manipulation (e.g., split()) to extract the name and age from each line.

Challenge 103: Find Lines Containing a Specific Word

Task: Write a Python function that reads a file and returns a list of all lines that contain a specific word.

```python
def find_lines_with_word(file_path, word):
    # Your code here
```

Hint: Use the in operator to check if the word exists in each line.

Challenge 104: Calculate the Average of Numbers in a File

Task: Write a Python function that reads a file where each line contains a number. The function should calculate and return the average of all the numbers in the file.

```python
def calculate_average(file_path):
    # Your code here
```

Hint: Convert each line to a number (e.g., using float() or int()) and calculate the sum and count of the numbers to compute the average.

Challenge 105: Process CSV Data and Calculate Statistics

Task: Write a Python function that reads a CSV file containing columns Name, Age, and Salary. The function should calculate the average salary and return it.

Example input (CSV format):

```
Name, Age, Salary
John, 25, 50000
Alice, 30, 60000
Bob, 22, 45000
python

import csv

def calculate_average_salary(file_path):
    # Your code here
```

Hint: Use the csv.reader module to read the CSV file and extract the salary values to compute the average.

Challenge 106: Convert CSV to Dictionary

Task: Write a Python function that reads a CSV file and returns a list of dictionaries. Each dictionary should represent a row in the CSV file with column names as the keys.

```
python

import csv

def csv_to_dict(file_path):
    # Your code here
```

Hint: Use the csv.DictReader class to read the CSV file directly into dictionaries.

Challenge 107: Filter Data from CSV

Task: Write a Python function that reads a CSV file containing employee information (e.g., Name, Department, Salary) and filters out employees with a salary less than a given value. The function should return a list of dictionaries containing the remaining employees.

```python
import csv

def filter_employees_by_salary(file_path, salary_threshold):
    # Your code here
```

Hint: Use the csv.DictReader to read the CSV and filter the rows based on salary.

Challenge 108: Merge Data from Two Files

Task: Write a Python function that reads two text files, each containing a list of names, and returns a single list with all names from both files, sorted alphabetically.

```python
def merge_and_sort_files(file_path1, file_path2):
    # Your code here
```

Hint: Read both files, merge their contents, and sort the resulting list using the sorted() function.

Challenge 109: Process and Format Data in a File

Task: Write a Python function that reads a file containing data in the format Name: Age: Score (e.g., John: 25: 90). The function should return a list of formatted strings like Name - Age: Score, sorted by score in descending order.

```python
```

WORKING WITH FILES AND BASIC DATA HANDLING

```python
def process_and_sort_data(file_path):
    # Your code here
```

Hint: Use string manipulation to extract the name, age, and score, then sort the data based on the score.

Challenge 110: Remove Empty Lines from a File

Task: Write a Python function that reads a file and removes all empty lines. The function should return a new file with the empty lines removed.

```python
def remove_empty_lines(input_file_path, output_file_path):
    # Your code here
```

Hint: Read all lines, filter out the empty lines, and write the remaining lines to a new file.

Solutions and Explanations

Below are solutions and explanations for each of the above challenges.

Solution to Challenge 101: Counting Word Frequency in a Text File

```python
from collections import Counter

def count_word_frequency(file_path):
    with open(file_path, 'r') as file:
        text = file.read().lower()  # Convert text to lowercase
        for case-insensitive counting
        words = text.split()
        word_count = Counter(words)
    return word_count
```

Explanation: This function reads the file's content, splits the text into words using split(), and counts each word's frequency using the Counter from the collections module.

Solution to Challenge 102: Extracting Specific Data from a File

python

```
def extract_name_age(file_path):
    result = []
    with open(file_path, 'r') as file:
        for line in file:
            name, age = line.strip().split(": ")
            result.append((name, int(age)))
    return result
```

Explanation: The function splits each line based on the colon and space, then converts the age to an integer and stores the name and age as a tuple.

Solution to Challenge 103: Find Lines Containing a Specific Word

python

```
def find_lines_with_word(file_path, word):
    result = []
    with open(file_path, 'r') as file:
        for line in file:
            if word in line:
                result.append(line.strip())
    return result
```

Explanation: This function reads each line of the file and checks if the specified word is in the line. If it is, the line is added to the result list.

Solution to Challenge 104: Calculate the Average of Numbers in a File

python

```
def calculate_average(file_path):
    total = 0
    count = 0
```

```
with open(file_path, 'r') as file:
    for line in file:
        total += float(line.strip())
        count += 1
return total / count if count != 0 else 0
```

Explanation: The function reads each line from the file, converts it to a float, and sums the numbers. It then calculates the average by dividing the total by the number of lines.

Solution to Challenge 105: Process CSV Data and Calculate Statistics

```python
import csv

def calculate_average_salary(file_path):
    total_salary = 0
    count = 0
    with open(file_path, 'r') as file:
        reader = csv.DictReader(file)
        for row in reader:
            total_salary += float(row['Salary'])
            count += 1
    return total_salary / count if count != 0 else 0
```

Explanation: This function uses the csv.DictReader to read the file and calculate the total salary, then computes the average by dividing the total salary by the number of rows.

Solution to Challenge 106: Convert CSV to Dictionary

```python
import csv

def csv_to_dict(file_path):
```

```
with open(file_path, 'r') as file:
    reader = csv.DictReader(file)
    return [row for row in reader]
```

Explanation: The csv.DictReader reads the file and converts each row into a dictionary where the keys are the column headers.

Solution to Challenge 107: Filter Data from CSV

python

```
import csv

def filter_employees_by_salary(file_path, salary_threshold):
    result = []
    with open(file_path, 'r') as file:
        reader = csv.DictReader(file)
        for row in reader:
            if float(row['Salary']) >= salary_threshold:
                result.append(row)
    return result
```

Explanation: This function reads the CSV file, and for each row, it checks if the salary exceeds the threshold. If so, it adds the row to the result list.

Solution to Challenge 108: Merge Data from Two Files

python

```
def merge_and_sort_files(file_path1, file_path2):
    with open(file_path1, 'r') as file1, open(file_path2, 'r') as file2:
        data = file1.readlines() + file2.readlines()
    return sorted(data)
```

Explanation: This function reads both files, merges their contents, and sorts the combined list alphabetically.

Solution to Challenge 109: Process and Format Data in a File

```python
def process_and_sort_data(file_path):
    data = []
    with open(file_path, 'r') as file:
        for line in file:
            name, age, score = line.strip().split(": ")
            data.append((name, int(age), int(score)))
    sorted_data = sorted(data, key=lambda x: x[2], reverse=True)
    return [f"{name} - {age}: {score}" for name, age, score in
    sorted_data]
```

Explanation: The function processes each line, splits the data into name, age, and score, and sorts the entries by score in descending order.

Solution to Challenge 110: Remove Empty Lines from a File

```python
def remove_empty_lines(input_file_path, output_file_path):
    with open(input_file_path, 'r') as input_file:
        lines = [line for line in input_file if line.strip()]
    with open(output_file_path, 'w') as output_file:
        output_file.writelines(lines)
```

Explanation: This function reads the input file, filters out the empty lines using a list comprehension, and writes the remaining lines to the output file.

These challenges help you develop a comprehensive understanding of processing data from files, including text manipulation, data analysis, and CSV handling. These are essential skills for anyone working with large datasets or handling data processing tasks in Python.

Solutions and Explanations for Challenges 91-110
Solution to Challenge 91: Reading a File Line by Line

python

```python
def read_file_line_by_line(file_path):
    with open(file_path, 'r') as file:
        for line in file:
            print(line.strip())
```

Explanation: This function opens the file and uses a for loop to read each line one at a time. The strip() method removes leading and trailing spaces or newlines from each line before printing. This is useful when you want to process large files line by line to conserve memory.

Solution to Challenge 92: Writing Data to a File

python

```python
def write_to_file(file_path, data):
    with open(file_path, 'w') as file:
        file.write(data)
```

Explanation: This function opens a file in write mode ('w'). It writes the provided data to the file. If the file does not exist, it will be created. If it already exists, it will be overwritten. This is helpful when you need to create or modify text files programmatically.

Solution to Challenge 93: Appending Data to an Existing File

python

```python
def append_to_file(file_path, data):
    with open(file_path, 'a') as file:
        file.write(data)
```

Explanation: This function opens the file in append mode ('a'), which allows new data to be added to the end of the file without overwriting the existing contents. It is useful when you want to keep adding data to a log file or continue appending entries over time.

Solution to Challenge 94: File Path Handling

WORKING WITH FILES AND BASIC DATA HANDLING

```python
import os

def handle_file_paths(file_path):
    print("File name:", os.path.basename(file_path))
    print("Directory:", os.path.dirname(file_path))
    print("Absolute path:", os.path.abspath(file_path))
```

Explanation: The function uses the os module to handle file paths. os.path.basename() returns the name of the file, os.path.dirname() gives the directory path, and os.path.abspath() returns the absolute file path. This is helpful when you need to manipulate or retrieve various parts of a file's path.

Solution to Challenge 95: Extracting Specific Columns from a CSV

```python
import csv

def extract_columns_from_csv(file_path, column_names):
    extracted_data = []
    with open(file_path, 'r') as file:
        reader = csv.DictReader(file)
        for row in reader:
            extracted_data.append({col: row[col] for col in
            column_names})
    return extracted_data
```

Explanation: This function uses csv.DictReader to read the CSV file as a dictionary, where the keys are column names. The function then filters out the specified columns and stores them in a new list. This is useful when you only need to extract a subset of data from a CSV file.

Solution to Challenge 96: Reading and Analyzing Numbers from a File

```python
def analyze_numbers_from_file(file_path):
    numbers = []
    with open(file_path, 'r') as file:
        for line in file:
            try:
                number = float(line.strip())
                numbers.append(number)
            except ValueError:
                continue  # Skip lines that are not numbers
    return sum(numbers), len(numbers), sum(numbers)/len(numbers)
    if numbers else 0
```

Explanation: This function reads each line of the file, tries to convert it to a float (ignoring lines that cannot be converted), and stores valid numbers in the numbers list. It then returns the sum, count, and average of the numbers. This is useful for analyzing numerical data from text files.

Solution to Challenge 97: Writing Data to a CSV File

```python
import csv

def write_to_csv(file_path, data, fieldnames):
    with open(file_path, 'w', newline='') as file:
        writer = csv.DictWriter(file, fieldnames=fieldnames)
        writer.writeheader()
        writer.writerows(data)
```

Explanation: This function uses csv.DictWriter to write data to a CSV file. It first writes the header using writeheader() and then writes the rows with writerows(). This is an efficient way to write dictionaries to CSV, especially when you have structured data.

Solution to Challenge 98: Searching for a Value in a CSV File

```python
import csv

def search_in_csv(file_path, search_term):
    found_rows = []
    with open(file_path, 'r') as file:
        reader = csv.DictReader(file)
        for row in reader:
            if search_term.lower() in str(row.values()).lower():
                found_rows.append(row)
    return found_rows
```

Explanation: This function reads the CSV file and checks if the search_term is present in any value of the row. The str(row.values()).lower() ensures that the search is case-insensitive. This is useful when you need to find rows containing a specific term across any column.

Solution to Challenge 99: Handling CSV with Missing Data

```python
import csv

def handle_missing_data(file_path):
    rows_with_missing_data = []
    with open(file_path, 'r') as file:
        reader = csv.DictReader(file)
        for row in reader:
            if '' in row.values():  # Check if any field is missing
                rows_with_missing_data.append(row)
    return rows_with_missing_data
```

Explanation: This function identifies rows in the CSV where any field is empty (missing data). It uses a check for an empty string '' in the row's values and collects rows with missing data. This is useful for cleaning and preprocessing data before further analysis.

Solution to Challenge 100: Modifying File Content (Replace Specific

Text)

```python
def modify_file_content(file_path, old_text, new_text):
    with open(file_path, 'r') as file:
        content = file.read()

    content = content.replace(old_text, new_text)

    with open(file_path, 'w') as file:
        file.write(content)
```

Explanation: This function reads the file content, replaces all occurrences of old_text with new_text, and writes the modified content back to the same file. This is helpful for updating or cleaning text files programmatically.

Solution to Challenge 101: Counting Word Frequency in a Text File

```python
from collections import Counter

def count_word_frequency(file_path):
    with open(file_path, 'r') as file:
        text = file.read().lower()   # Convert text to lowercase
                                     # for case-insensitive counting
        words = text.split()
        word_count = Counter(words)
    return word_count
```

Explanation: This function reads the entire file, converts the content to lowercase for case-insensitive word counting, splits the text into individual words using split(), and counts the occurrences using Counter from the collections module. This helps you analyze how often each word appears in the text.

Solution to Challenge 102: Extracting Specific Data from a File

WORKING WITH FILES AND BASIC DATA HANDLING

```python
def extract_name_age(file_path):
    result = []
    with open(file_path, 'r') as file:
        for line in file:
            name, age = line.strip().split(": ")
            result.append((name, int(age)))
    return result
```

Explanation: This function splits each line of the file at : to separate the name and age, and converts the age into an integer before appending the data as a tuple to the result list. It is useful for extracting structured data from a text file where the format is consistent.

Solution to Challenge 103: Find Lines Containing a Specific Word

```python
def find_lines_with_word(file_path, word):
    result = []
    with open(file_path, 'r') as file:
        for line in file:
            if word in line:
                result.append(line.strip())
    return result
```

Explanation: This function reads each line from the file and checks if the given word exists in the line. If found, the line is added to the result list. This is useful when searching for specific terms in a text file.

Solution to Challenge 104: Calculate the Average of Numbers in a File

```python
def calculate_average(file_path):
    total = 0
```

```
    count = 0
    with open(file_path, 'r') as file:
        for line in file:
            total += float(line.strip())
            count += 1
    return total / count if count != 0 else 0
```

Explanation: The function reads each line of the file, converts the content to a float, and adds it to a running total. It then divides the total by the number of lines to calculate the average. This is a simple way to process numerical data from a text file.

These solutions provide hands-on experience with file handling, text processing, and basic data analysis using Python. By working through these challenges, you gain practical skills that will be helpful for real-world data processing tasks.

Mini Project 5: "Simple Data Logger"

In this mini project, we will create a simple data logger in Python that can log user input to a file. The logger will continuously capture data (such as temperature readings, sensor data, or other numerical inputs), append them to a log file, and provide basic feedback to the user. This is a great way to practice file handling, input processing, and time management with Python.

Project Requirements:

1. The user will be prompted to enter a piece of data (e.g., a temperature reading).
2. The program will timestamp the data entry.
3. The program will append the data to a log file.
4. The user will have the option to stop logging or continue.
5. The data should be formatted in a clear way, showing the timestamp and the logged value.

Step 1: Create the Logger Script

WORKING WITH FILES AND BASIC DATA HANDLING

The first step is to write a Python script that prompts the user for input and logs it to a file.

```python
import datetime

def log_data(log_file):
    while True:
        # Prompt the user for input
        data = input("Enter data to log (or type 'exit' to stop): ")

        # Exit condition
        if data.lower() == 'exit':
            print("Exiting data logger.")
            break

        # Get the current timestamp
        timestamp = datetime.datetime.now().strftime("%Y-%m-%d %H:%M:%S")

        # Log the data to a file
        with open(log_file, 'a') as file:
            file.write(f"{timestamp}    {data}\n")

        # Provide feedback to the user
        print(f"Data logged: {timestamp} - {data}")

# Call the log_data function to start logging
log_data("data_log.txt")
```

Explanation of Code:
Imports:

- datetime is imported to capture the current date and time, which will be used as a timestamp for each log entry.

log_data function:

- The function runs in an infinite loop, repeatedly prompting the user for data until they type 'exit' to stop the logging.
- For each entry, the current date and time are captured using datetime. datetime.now() and formatted to YYYY-MM-DD HH:MM:SS.
- The data, along with the timestamp, is appended to the log file. We use 'a' mode to append to the file rather than overwriting it.
- The input function is used to get user input. If the user types 'exit', the loop breaks and the program ends.

Logging the Data:

- Each entry in the log file is saved in the format: timestamp - data. Each new entry is appended on a new line.

Stopping the Program:

- If the user types 'exit', the program stops logging and exits.

Step 2: Enhance the Data Logger with Input Validation

You may want to ensure that the input meets certain criteria, for example, only logging numerical values or adding units to the logged data. Here's how you can modify the script to handle input validation.

python

```
import datetime

def log_data_with_validation(log_file):
    while True:
        # Prompt the user for input
        data = input("Enter numerical data to log (or type 'exit' to stop): ")

        # Exit condition
```

WORKING WITH FILES AND BASIC DATA HANDLING

```python
        if data.lower() == 'exit':
            print("Exiting data logger.")
            break

        # Input validation to check if the data is a valid number
        try:
            float_data = float(data)
        except ValueError:
            print("Invalid input! Please enter a numerical
            value.")
            continue

        # Get the current timestamp
        timestamp = datetime.datetime.now().strftime("%Y-%m-%d
        %H:%M:%S")

        # Log the data to a file
        with open(log_file, 'a') as file:
            file.write(f"{timestamp} - {float_data}\n")

        # Provide feedback to the user
        print(f"Data logged: {timestamp} - {float_data}")

# Call the log_data_with_validation function to start logging
log_data_with_validation("data_log.txt")
```

Enhancements Explained:
Input Validation:

- A try-except block is used to check whether the user's input can be converted to a float. If the input is not a valid number, the program informs the user and prompts them to try again.
- This ensures that only numerical values are logged, making the program more robust and less prone to invalid entries.

Feedback:

- If the input is valid, the data is logged with the timestamp, and the user is given feedback with the logged entry.

Step 3: Adding a Simple Report Function

To make the data logger more useful, you could add functionality to generate a simple report of the logged data. This could include reading the log file and displaying the entries in a readable format.

```python
def generate_report(log_file):
    print("\nGenerating Report from Log File...\n")

    try:
        with open(log_file, 'r') as file:
            lines = file.readlines()

            if not lines:
                print("No data found in the log file.")
                return

            # Display all entries in the log
            for line in lines:
                print(line.strip())

    except FileNotFoundError:
        print(f"Error: The log file '{log_file}' does not exist.")

# Call the generate_report function
generate_report("data_log.txt")
```

Explanation of the Report Generation:
Reading the Log File:

- The generate_report function opens the log file in read mode ('r') and reads all lines.
- If the file is empty, a message is displayed informing the user that there is no data.

Handling Missing Log Files:

- If the log file does not exist, a FileNotFoundError is handled gracefully by displaying an error message.

Displaying Log Entries:

- Each line of the log file is printed, showing the timestamp and the corresponding data entry.

Putting It All Together:
Now you have a working data logger with validation and a report generation feature. The program first logs data with timestamps, validates user input, and then allows the user to generate reports of the logged data.

This simple data logger project teaches important file handling skills, including appending data to files, input validation, and generating reports from the data. It demonstrates how you can combine user input, file handling, and data processing to create a useful tool for logging and analyzing data in Python.

Possible Extensions:
- **Data Filtering:** Implement functionality to filter data based on certain conditions (e.g., only log entries above a certain value).
- **Log File Rotation:** Create a system that rotates log files when they grow too large, ensuring the program remains efficient and manageable.
- **Data Visualization:** Incorporate a simple chart or graph generation using libraries like matplotlib to visualize the logged data.

Test Your Knowledge: File Handling Quiz
After exploring the fundamentals of file handling in Python, it's essential

to test your understanding of the concepts and techniques learned. Below is a quiz designed to assess your knowledge of reading from and writing to files, handling file paths, and processing data within files.

1. What is the correct mode for opening a file for reading in Python?
A) 'w'
B) 'r'
C) 'a'
D) 'x'

2. Which of the following methods can be used to read the entire contents of a file in Python?
A) file.read()
B) file.readline()
C) file.readlines()
D) Both A and C

3. What happens if you attempt to open a file in write mode ('w') when the file does not already exist?
A) Python raises an error.
B) Python creates a new file and writes to it.
C) Python does nothing and returns None.
D) Python creates a new file but only allows reading.

4. How can you ensure that a file is automatically closed after its contents are processed?
A) By manually calling file.close().
B) By using the with statement to open the file.
C) By using file.flush() after every write.
D) By opening the file in 'a' mode.

5. What does the 'a' mode do when opening a file?
A) Opens the file for reading.
B) Opens the file for writing, but only if the file exists.

C) Appends to the file, creating the file if it doesn't exist.
D) Opens the file for writing and overwrites it.

6. What is the default encoding when opening a file in Python without specifying one?
A) 'utf-8'
B) 'ascii'
C) 'latin-1'
D) None (Python chooses automatically based on the system)

7. Which of the following is correct for reading a file line by line in Python?
A) file.read(1)
B) file.readline()
C) file.readlines()
D) Both B and C

8. How would you open a file in read mode and print each line individually using a loop?
A)

```python
with open('file.txt', 'r') as file:
    for line in file:
        print(line)
```

B)

```python
file = open('file.txt', 'r')
for line in file:
    print(line)
```

C)

```python
with open('file.txt', 'r') as file:
    print(file.read())
```

D)

```python
open('file.txt', 'r') as file:
    for line in file:
        print(line)
```

9. Which method would you use to write a string to a file in Python?
A) file.write()
B) file.append()
C) file.write_string()
D) file.add()

10. What happens when you try to read from a file that is already closed?
A) Python raises an IOError.
B) Python automatically reopens the file for reading.
C) Python will read the last line accessed.
D) Python returns an empty string.

11. How can you append text to an existing file in Python?
A) Open the file in 'r' mode and use file.write().
B) Open the file in 'w' mode and use file.write().
C) Open the file in 'a' mode and use file.write().
D) Open the file in 'x' mode and use file.write().

12. What is the difference between read() and readlines() methods?

A) read() returns the entire content as a list, while readlines() returns the entire content as a string.

B) read() reads the entire file content as a string, while readlines() reads the content and returns a list of lines.

C) read() and readlines() are identical methods.

D) readlines() reads a single line at a time, while read() reads the entire file.

13. Which of the following is true about file paths in Python?

A) File paths are always relative by default.

B) Absolute file paths can be specified, but relative file paths are not allowed.

C) Both absolute and relative file paths can be used in Python, with relative paths being the default.

D) File paths must always start with C: on Windows or / on Linux.

14. What does the with statement provide when handling files in Python?

A) Ensures that the file is written and closed automatically, even if an error occurs.

B) Automatically handles file encoding.

C) Allows you to read from and write to the same file at the same time.

D) Guarantees that the file is always opened in append mode.

15. When working with binary files, which method is used to read or write data?

A) file.read()

B) file.read(1)

C) file.readall()

D) file.read() opened in binary mode ('rb' or 'wb')

Answer Key:

1. B) 'r'
2. D) Both A and C
3. B) Python creates a new file and writes to it.
4. B) By using the with statement to open the file.
5. C) Appends to the file, creating the file if it doesn't exist.
6. A) 'utf-8'
7. D) Both B and C
8. A)
9. A) file.write()
10. A) Python raises an IOError.
11. C) Open the file in 'a' mode and use file.write().
12. B) read() reads the entire file content as a string, while readlines() reads the content and returns a list of lines.
13. C) Both absolute and relative file paths can be used in Python, with relative paths being the default.
14. A) Ensures that the file is written and closed automatically, even if an error occurs.
15. D) file.read() opened in binary mode ('rb' or 'wb')

This quiz tests your fundamental knowledge of file handling in Python, including reading, writing, appending, and managing file paths. After completing the quiz, review the answers to solidify your understanding of file handling and data processing.

Debugging and Optimization

Overview: Finding and Fixing Common Errors

As you progress in programming, the inevitability of encountering bugs—errors or issues within your code—is a natural part of the development process. These bugs can range from simple syntax mistakes to more complex logical errors that can be hard to trace. Debugging, the process of identifying, isolating, and fixing these errors, is a critical skill for any programmer.

Understanding common errors and knowing how to efficiently identify and fix them is essential for writing reliable, efficient, and maintainable code. This chapter will provide you with the tools, techniques, and strategies to handle errors in Python, as well as best practices for debugging and optimizing your code.

Types of Errors in Python

Before diving into debugging strategies, it's important to understand the different types of errors that you might encounter while programming in Python. Errors can be classified into the following categories:

Syntax Errors

Syntax errors are the simplest to detect but can be frustrating. They occur when Python cannot interpret your code because it violates the grammar of the language. These errors are usually caught at compile-time, meaning that they prevent the program from running at all.

Examples:

```python
print("Hello, World!)   # Missing closing quote
if x == 10 print(x)    # Missing colon after 'if'
```

Runtime Errors

Runtime errors occur while the program is running. These errors are usually caused by invalid operations, such as dividing by zero, accessing a non-existent list index, or trying to open a file that doesn't exist. Python raises exceptions in these situations, and if not handled properly, the program will crash.

Examples:

```python
x = 10 / 0   # Division by zero
my_list = [1, 2, 3]
print(my_list[5])   # Index out of range
```

Logical Errors

Logical errors are the most difficult to identify because the code runs without raising any exceptions. These errors occur when the program produces an incorrect result due to a mistake in the logic of the code. The program may run successfully, but the output is not what you expected.

Example:

```python
def add_numbers(a, b):
    return a * b  # Logical error: should be addition, not
    multiplication
```

Exception Handling

Python provides a mechanism for handling runtime errors through exceptions. Exceptions are raised when an error occurs, and they can be caught and handled using a try-except block. This allows you to write more robust and error-resilient programs.

Example:

python

```
try:
    value = int(input("Enter a number: "))
except ValueError:
    print("Invalid input, please enter a valid number.")
```

Debugging Strategies

Now that we understand the types of errors, let's explore various strategies for debugging Python code effectively.

1. Using Print Statements

One of the simplest and most effective debugging techniques is inserting print() statements at key points in your code. These statements allow you to track the flow of execution and inspect the values of variables at different stages.

Example:

python

```
def calculate_area(length, width):
    print(f"Length: {length}, Width: {width}")   # Debugging print
    area = length * width
    print(f"Area: {area}")   # Debugging print
    return area

calculate_area(5, 10)
```

While this method is quick and simple, it can clutter your code and might not be ideal for larger or more complex projects. Nonetheless, it can be very helpful for tracking down issues in small scripts or during initial development.

2. Using Python's Built-in Debugger (pdb)

Python includes a powerful debugger called pdb (Python Debugger), which allows you to step through your code line by line, inspect variables, and interact with your program during execution.

To use pdb, you simply import the module and set a breakpoint using pdb.set_trace() where you want the debugger to pause.

Example:

```python
import pdb

def divide_numbers(a, b):
    pdb.set_trace()   # Set a breakpoint
    return a / b

result = divide_numbers(10, 2)
```

Once the breakpoint is hit, you can type commands in the terminal to inspect variables (print(variable)), continue execution (c), step to the next line (n), or exit the debugger (q).

pdb is invaluable when you need to examine the program's state during execution and pinpoint exactly where things go wrong.

3. Using IDE Debugger Tools

Many integrated development environments (IDEs), such as PyCharm, Visual Studio Code, or even Jupyter Notebooks, come with built-in debuggers that provide a graphical interface for stepping through code, inspecting variables, and setting breakpoints. These tools are often more intuitive than using pdb directly and are excellent for larger projects.

Using the IDE's debugger, you can set breakpoints, step through code, view the call stack, and modify variable values in real-time.

4. Code Reviews and Pair Programming

Sometimes, the best way to debug an issue is to get a fresh pair of eyes on your code. Code reviews and pair programming are valuable practices for catching errors, improving code quality, and optimizing logic. When someone else reads your code, they are more likely to spot issues that you might overlook after working on it for a while.

During pair programming, two programmers work together at the same computer: one writes the code while the other reviews it. This collaborative approach helps identify mistakes early in the development process.

5. Using Unit Testing and Test-Driven Development (TDD)

Unit testing involves writing small tests for individual functions or modules in your program to ensure they behave as expected. By writing tests before or alongside your code (a practice known as Test-Driven Development, or TDD), you can catch errors early in the development cycle.

Python provides the unittest module, which you can use to create test cases for your code.

Example:

```python
import unittest

def add_numbers(a, b):
    return a + b

class TestMathOperations(unittest.TestCase):
    def test_add_numbers(self):
        self.assertEqual(add_numbers(2, 3), 5)

if __name__ == "__main__":
    unittest.main()
```

In this example, the test_add_numbers() method ensures that the add_numbers() function correctly adds two values. Running the test will tell you if your function passes or fails. Unit testing allows you to isolate individual parts of your code and test them independently, which is especially useful for complex projects.

Optimization Strategies

Once you've identified and fixed errors, the next step is to optimize your code. Optimizing code means making it more efficient, faster, and memory-friendly while maintaining or improving its readability. Below are some key strategies for optimization:

1. Algorithm Optimization

Before optimizing the syntax of your code, make sure the algorithm itself is as efficient as possible. For example, instead of using a brute-force approach to solve a problem, consider alternative algorithms that might be more time-efficient.

Example: A common algorithmic optimization is switching from a nested loop to a more efficient search or sorting algorithm, such as a binary search or merge sort.

2. Using Built-In Python Functions

Python's standard library includes a rich set of optimized functions that can often replace custom code, leading to significant performance improvements. Whenever possible, use built-in functions instead of writing your own.

For example, using Python's built-in sum() to sum a list of numbers is faster than manually iterating through the list and adding them up.

Example:

```python
numbers = [1, 2, 3, 4, 5]
total = sum(numbers)   # Optimized built-in function
```

3. Profiling Code

DEBUGGING AND OPTIMIZATION

Profiling is the process of measuring the performance of your code to find bottlenecks. Python provides a cProfile module to help you analyze the performance of your program and identify areas that can be optimized.

Example:

```python
import cProfile

def slow_function():
    result = 0
    for i in range(1000000):
        result += i
    return result

cProfile.run('slow_function()')
```

The cProfile module outputs a performance report, showing how much time each function call takes and how often it is called. This information can guide your optimization efforts.

4. Efficient Data Structures

Choosing the right data structure can have a significant impact on the performance of your program. For instance, using a dictionary (hash map) for lookups is much faster than using a list. Similarly, using sets for membership tests is more efficient than using lists.

Example:

```python
# Using a set for faster membership checks
my_set = {1, 2, 3}
if 2 in my_set:
    print("Found!")
```

5. Memory Management

Optimizing memory usage is essential for performance, especially in large applications. Avoid unnecessary copies of large data structures, use generators instead of lists where possible, and consider using more memory-efficient data types, such as array for numeric data.

Debugging and optimization are crucial steps in the software development process. By mastering techniques like print statements, pdb, unit testing, and algorithmic improvements, you can identify and fix errors more efficiently, leading to cleaner and more efficient code. In addition, optimizing your code by using Python's built-in functions, profiling tools, and proper data structures will result in faster, more memory-efficient programs. Debugging is a skill that improves with practice, and the more experience you gain, the more adept you'll become at writing clean and optimized code.

Challenge 111-120: Identifying and Resolving Errors

Topics: Syntax errors, logic errors, debugging techniques

Debugging is an essential skill for any programmer. The ability to identify and resolve errors in your code quickly will save you time and improve the quality of your programs. In this section, we will present several coding challenges that focus on different types of errors—syntax errors, logic errors, and debugging techniques—and provide strategies for resolving them.

Challenge 111: Fix the Syntax Error in the Code
Problem:
The following code contains a syntax error. Your task is to identify the error and correct it so the code runs successfully.

```python
def greet(name):
    print("Hello, " + name)

greet("Alice"
```

Hint: Pay attention to parentheses.

Solution:

The issue here is a missing closing parenthesis for the function call greet("Alice"). To fix this error, simply add the closing parenthesis:

```python
def greet(name):
    print("Hello, " + name)

greet("Alice")
```

Challenge 112: Resolve the Indentation Error
Problem:

In Python, indentation is very important for defining code blocks. The following code will result in an indentation error. Identify the mistake and correct it.

```python
def calculate_total(price, tax):
total = price + (price * tax)
return total

print(calculate_total(100, 0.07))
```

Hint: Ensure the code inside the function is indented properly.

Solution:

The code inside the calculate_total function needs to be indented correctly. Here's the corrected version:

python

```
def calculate_total(price, tax):
    total = price + (price * tax)
    return total

print(calculate_total(100, 0.07))
```

Challenge 113: Correct the Logical Error
Problem:

This function is intended to check if a number is even or odd, but it contains a logical error. Identify the mistake and correct it.

python

```
def check_even_odd(number):
    if number % 2 = 0:
        return "Even"
    else:
        return "Odd"

print(check_even_odd(4))
```

Hint: Look at the comparison operator.
Solution:

The issue is that the = operator is used, which is the assignment operator, rather than the equality comparison operator ==. Here's the corrected code:

python

```
def check_even_odd(number):
    if number % 2 == 0:
```

DEBUGGING AND OPTIMIZATION

```
        return "Even"
    else:
        return "Odd"

print(check_even_odd(4))
```

Challenge 114: Fix the NameError
Problem:

This code results in a NameError because a variable is used before it is defined. Find the error and fix it.

python

```
def calculate_area(radius):
    area = pi * (radius ** 2)
    return area

print(calculate_area(5))
```

Hint: Check if all the variables are defined before they are used.

Solution:

The error occurs because the variable pi is used without being defined. To resolve this, you need to define pi before using it:

python

```
def calculate_area(radius):
    pi = 3.14159
    area = pi * (radius ** 2)
    return area

print(calculate_area(5))
```

Challenge 115: Resolve the TypeError
Problem:

This code results in a TypeError when you try to add a string and an integer. Identify and fix the error.

python

```
def add_numbers(a, b):
    return a + b

print(add_numbers("Hello", 5))
```

Hint: Check the data types of the operands.

Solution:

The problem is that you are trying to add a string and an integer, which is not allowed in Python. You can fix the issue by either converting the integer to a string or the string to an integer (depending on the intended behavior). Here's how you can fix it by converting the integer to a string:

python

```
def add_numbers(a, b):
    return a + str(b)

print(add_numbers("Hello", 5))
```

Alternatively, you can convert the string to an integer if the string contains a valid number:

python

```
def add_numbers(a, b):
    return int(a) + b

print(add_numbers("5", 5))
```

Challenge 116: Fix the IndexError
Problem:

DEBUGGING AND OPTIMIZATION

The following code results in an IndexError because the list index is out of range. Identify and fix the error.

```python
my_list = [1, 2, 3]
print(my_list[3])
```

Hint: Ensure you are accessing valid indices in the list.

Solution:

The issue is that you are trying to access the element at index 3, but the list only has elements at indices 0, 1, and 2. To fix this, you can change the index to a valid value:

```python
my_list = [1, 2, 3]
print(my_list[2])  # Access the last element
```

Challenge 117: Resolve the ValueError

Problem:

This code raises a ValueError when attempting to convert a string to an integer. Identify and correct the error.

```python
def convert_to_integer(value):
    return int(value)

print(convert_to_integer("abc"))
```

Hint: Think about how to handle invalid input.

Solution:

The error occurs because the string "abc" cannot be converted to an integer. To handle this, we can add error handling using a try-except block:

```python
def convert_to_integer(value):
    try:
        return int(value)
    except ValueError:
        return "Invalid input"

print(convert_to_integer("abc"))
```

This will catch the ValueError and return a more user-friendly message.

Challenge 118: Debug the Infinite Loop
Problem:
The following code creates an infinite loop. Identify the cause and fix the loop.

```python
def count_up_to(limit):
    number = 1
    while number <= limit:
        print(number)
        # Missing increment of number
```

Hint: Ensure that the loop's condition is eventually met.
Solution:
The issue is that the value of number is never updated within the loop, so it will always be 1, causing the loop to run infinitely. To fix this, increment number inside the loop:

```python
def count_up_to(limit):
    number = 1
```

```
    while number <= limit:
        print(number)
        number += 1  # Increment the number

count_up_to(5)
```

Challenge 119: Fix the KeyError
Problem:

This code throws a KeyError because the key is not found in the dictionary. Identify the issue and fix it.

```python
my_dict = {"name": "Alice", "age": 25}
print(my_dict["address"])
```

Hint: Ensure that the key exists in the dictionary before accessing it.
Solution:

The problem is that the key "address" does not exist in the dictionary. You can fix this by using the get() method, which will return None if the key does not exist:

```python
my_dict = {"name": "Alice", "age": 25}
print(my_dict.get("address", "Key not found"))
```

Alternatively, you could check for the key before accessing it:

```python
my_dict = {"name": "Alice", "age": 25}
if "address" in my_dict:
    print(my_dict["address"])
else:
```

```
    print("Key not found")
```

Challenge 120: Fix the OverflowError
Problem:

The following code results in an OverflowError when trying to multiply large numbers. Identify and correct the error.

```python
def multiply_large_numbers(a, b):
    return a * b

print(multiply_large_numbers(1e100, 1e100))
```

Hint: Think about large numbers and their limits in Python.

Solution:

Python's floating-point numbers have limits on how large they can be. When multiplying large numbers, an OverflowError can occur. One possible fix is to use Python's decimal module, which can handle arbitrarily large numbers with more precision:

```python
from decimal import Decimal

def multiply_large_numbers(a, b):
    return a * b

print(multiply_large_numbers(Decimal(1e100), Decimal(1e100)))
```

These challenges highlight common errors such as syntax errors, logical errors, and runtime exceptions that developers encounter in everyday programming. By solving these problems, you'll improve your debugging skills and become more efficient at identifying and fixing issues in your code. Remember, debugging is a critical skill, and with practice, you'll become faster at resolving errors and writing robust code.

Challenge 121-130: Code Optimization

Topics: Time complexity basics, improving code efficiency, refactoring

Optimizing code is an essential part of writing efficient programs, particularly when working with large datasets or complex algorithms. The goal of optimization is not only to make code run faster but also to improve its readability and maintainability. In this section, we will present challenges that focus on improving the efficiency of existing code, understanding time complexity, and refactoring code for better performance.

Challenge 121: Optimize the Loop with a Better Approach

Problem:

The following code uses a nested loop to search for duplicates in a list. This approach is inefficient, especially with large datasets. Your task is to optimize the code.

```python
def find_duplicates(arr):
    duplicates = []
    for i in range(len(arr)):
        for j in range(i + 1, len(arr)):
            if arr[i] == arr[j] and arr[i] not in duplicates:
                duplicates.append(arr[i])
    return duplicates
```

```python
print(find_duplicates([1, 2, 3, 2, 4, 5, 1, 6, 7]))
```

Hint: Think about how to check for duplicates more efficiently.

Solution:

The current solution has a time complexity of O(n^2) because of the nested loops. A more efficient solution would involve using a set to keep track of seen elements. This reduces the time complexity to O(n):

python

```python
def find_duplicates(arr):
    seen = set()
    duplicates = set()
    for num in arr:
        if num in seen:
            duplicates.add(num)
        else:
            seen.add(num)
    return list(duplicates)

print(find_duplicates([1, 2, 3, 2, 4, 5, 1, 6, 7]))
```

This solution is much more efficient because the set operations (checking membership and adding elements) are O(1) on average.

Challenge 122: Refactor Code for Better Readability

Problem:

The following code is functional but can be refactored for improved readability and structure. Your task is to refactor it.

python

```python
def calculate_discount(price, discount):
    discounted_price = price - price * (discount / 100)
    if discounted_price < 0:
```

DEBUGGING AND OPTIMIZATION

```
        discounted_price = 0
    return discounted_price

def calculate_tax(price, tax_rate):
    return price * (tax_rate / 100)

def calculate_total(price, discount, tax_rate):
    price_after_discount = calculate_discount(price, discount)
    tax = calculate_tax(price_after_discount, tax_rate)
    total_price = price_after_discount + tax
    return total_price

print(calculate_total(100, 20, 8))
```

Hint: Look for repetitive code and try to combine logic where appropriate.

Solution:

We can refactor the code by making it more modular and easier to maintain, without repeating code for calculating the discount and tax. Here's a refactored version:

```python
def apply_percentage(value, percentage):
    return value * (percentage / 100)

def calculate_total(price, discount, tax_rate):
    price_after_discount = price - apply_percentage(price, discount)
    price_after_tax = price_after_discount + apply_percentage(price_after_discount, tax_rate)
    return max(price_after_tax, 0)

print(calculate_total(100, 20, 8))
```

By combining the discount and tax calculation into a single function apply_percentage, we've reduced redundancy and improved the clarity of the logic.

Challenge 123: Improve the Algorithm for Sorting
Problem:

The following code uses a basic bubble sort algorithm to sort a list. While bubble sort is functional, it is inefficient for larger datasets. Refactor the code to improve sorting performance.

python

```
def bubble_sort(arr):
    for i in range(len(arr)):
        for j in range(0, len(arr) - i - 1):
            if arr[j] > arr[j + 1]:
                arr[j], arr[j + 1] = arr[j + 1], arr[j]
    return arr

print(bubble_sort([64, 34, 25, 12, 22, 11, 90]))
```

Hint: Consider using a more efficient sorting algorithm.

Solution:

Bubble sort has a time complexity of $O(n^2)$, which can be inefficient for large datasets. We can replace it with a more efficient sorting algorithm, such as quicksort or Python's built-in sorted() function, which has a time complexity of $O(n \log n)$:

python

```
def quicksort(arr):
    if len(arr) <= 1:
        return arr
    pivot = arr[0]
    less = [x for x in arr[1:] if x <= pivot]
    greater = [x for x in arr[1:] if x > pivot]
    return quicksort(less) + [pivot] + quicksort(greater)

print(quicksort([64, 34, 25, 12, 22, 11, 90]))
```

Or, you can take advantage of Python's optimized sorting method:

```python
def optimized_sort(arr):
    return sorted(arr)

print(optimized_sort([64, 34, 25, 12, 22, 11, 90]))
```

This significantly improves the performance for large lists.

Challenge 124: Optimize a Search Algorithm
Problem:
The following code uses a linear search to find an item in a list. Optimize it by using a more efficient algorithm.

```python
def linear_search(arr, target):
    for i in range(len(arr)):
        if arr[i] == target:
            return i
    return -1

print(linear_search([5, 2, 9, 1, 5, 6], 9))
```

Hint: Look into binary search if the list is sorted.
Solution:
The linear search has a time complexity of O(n), but if the list is sorted, you can use binary search to improve the search time to O(log n). Here's an implementation of binary search:

```python
def binary_search(arr, target):
    left, right = 0, len(arr) - 1
    while left <= right:
```

```
        mid = (left + right) // 2
        if arr[mid] == target:
            return mid
        elif arr[mid] < target:
            left = mid + 1
        else:
            right = mid - 1
    return -1

# Ensure the list is sorted first
arr = [1, 2, 5, 5, 6, 9]
print(binary_search(arr, 9))
```

Binary search works only with sorted data, but it is much faster than linear search for large lists.

Challenge 125: Improve Memory Usage in a Function
Problem:
The following code creates a new list of squares of numbers. However, it uses extra memory by storing the entire list in memory at once. Refactor the code to make it more memory-efficient.

python

```
def generate_squares(n):
    squares = []
    for i in range(n):
        squares.append(i ** 2)
    return squares

print(generate_squares(1000000))
```

Hint: Consider using a generator to avoid storing large lists in memory.
Solution:
Instead of storing all the squares in memory at once, we can use a generator, which produces values one at a time. This approach will reduce memory usage significantly:

DEBUGGING AND OPTIMIZATION

```python
def generate_squares(n):
    for i in range(n):
        yield i ** 2

squares_generator = generate_squares(1000000)
for square in squares_generator:
    if square > 100:    # Just print the first few squares
        break
```

Using yield creates a generator that yields one value at a time, avoiding the need to store the entire list in memory.

Challenge 126: Refactor a Recursive Function for Efficiency
Problem:
The following code calculates the Fibonacci sequence using recursion. However, it is inefficient due to redundant calculations. Refactor the function for better performance.

```python
def fibonacci(n):
    if n <= 1:
        return n
    return fibonacci(n - 1) + fibonacci(n - 2)

print(fibonacci(35))
```

Hint: Consider using memoization to store previously calculated results.
Solution:
The recursive Fibonacci function has a time complexity of $O(2^n)$ because it recalculates the same values multiple times. We can use memoization to store the results of previous function calls, reducing the time complexity

to O(n):

```python
def fibonacci(n, memo={}):
    if n <= 1:
        return n
    if n not in memo:
        memo[n] = fibonacci(n - 1, memo) + fibonacci(n - 2, memo)
    return memo[n]

print(fibonacci(35))
```

Memoization caches the results of previous function calls, so each Fibonacci number is calculated only once.

Challenge 127: Simplify a Complex Expression
Problem:

The following code contains a complex expression that can be simplified. Your task is to refactor it for readability and performance.

```python
def calculate_price(price, discount, tax):
    return (price - price * (discount / 100)) * (1 + (tax / 100))

print(calculate_price(100, 20, 8))
```

Hint: Look for opportunities to break the expression into smaller, more understandable parts.

Solution:

We can break down the expression into smaller steps to make it more readable and easier to understand:

```python
def calculate_price(price, discount, tax):
    price_after_discount = price - (price * (discount / 100))
    total_price = price_after_discount * (1 + (tax / 100))
    return total_price

print(calculate_price(100, 20, 8))
```

This makes the logic clearer and easier to follow.

Challenge 128: Reduce Redundant Calculations
Problem:
The following code has redundant calculations that can be optimized. Refactor it to remove the repetition.

```python
def calculate_area(radius):
    return 3.14159 * radius ** 2

def calculate_circumference(radius):
    return 2 * 3.14159 * radius

def calculate(radius):
    area = calculate_area(radius)
    circumference = calculate_circumference(radius)
    return area, circumference

print(calculate(5))
```

Hint: Can you calculate both area and circumference in one function call to reduce repeated calculations?

Solution:
We can calculate both the area and circumference in a single function call to avoid redundant computation of 3.14159 * radius. Here's the refactored code:

```python
def calculate(radius):
    pi = 3.14159
    area = pi * radius ** 2
    circumference = 2 * pi * radius
    return area, circumference

print(calculate(5))
```

This eliminates the need for repeated calculation of the constant value 3.14159.

Challenge 129: Optimize Sorting for Large Datasets
Problem:
The following code sorts a large dataset using the inefficient bubble sort algorithm. Refactor the code to use a more efficient sorting method.

```python
def bubble_sort(arr):
    for i in range(len(arr)):
        for j in range(0, len(arr) - i - 1):
            if arr[j] > arr[j + 1]:
                arr[j], arr[j + 1] = arr[j + 1], arr[j]
    return arr

# Simulating a large dataset
data = list(range(1000000, 0, -1))
bubble_sort(data)
```

Hint: Use Python's built-in sorting method for efficiency.
Solution:
Instead of using bubble sort, we can use Python's built-in sorted() function, which is optimized and runs in O(n log n) time:

```python
data = list(range(1000000, 0, -1))
sorted_data = sorted(data)
```

This is significantly more efficient for large datasets.

Challenge 130: Optimize Memory Usage for Large Data

Problem:

The following code processes a large list of numbers. It uses a list to store intermediate results, leading to high memory usage. Refactor the code to improve memory efficiency.

```python
def process_numbers(numbers):
    results = []
    for num in numbers:
        results.append(num ** 2)
    return results

numbers = list(range(1000000))
processed_numbers = process_numbers(numbers)
```

Hint: Consider using a generator to avoid storing intermediate results in memory.

Solution:

By using a generator, we can avoid storing the intermediate list in memory:

```python
def process_numbers(numbers):
    for num in numbers:
```

```
    yield num ** 2

numbers = list(range(1000000))
processed_numbers = process_numbers(numbers)
```

The generator will yield one squared number at a time, significantly reducing memory usage.

These challenges focus on improving code efficiency through better algorithms, refactoring, and memory optimization. By optimizing your code, you can handle larger datasets, improve runtime, and make your programs more efficient and scalable.

Solutions and Explanations

Below are the detailed solutions and explanations for the challenges presented in **Challenge 121–130** on code optimization. Each challenge presents a scenario where the code could be improved either by optimizing the algorithm, refactoring for readability, reducing redundancy, or managing memory more effectively. Let's go over each one to help you better understand the approach and reasoning behind the optimizations.

Challenge 121: Optimize the Loop with a Better Approach

Original Solution: The original solution uses nested loops to search for duplicates in the list, which is inefficient with a time complexity of $O(n^2)$. Here's the original code:

python

```
def find_duplicates(arr):
    duplicates = []
    for i in range(len(arr)):
        for j in range(i + 1, len(arr)):
            if arr[i] == arr[j] and arr[i] not in duplicates:
                duplicates.append(arr[i])
    return duplicates
```

Optimized Solution: We can optimize the algorithm by using a set, which

DEBUGGING AND OPTIMIZATION

allows for O(1) average time complexity for checking membership. This improves the overall time complexity from O(n^2) to O(n), as we only need to loop through the array once:

python

```
def find_duplicates(arr):
    seen = set()
    duplicates = set()
    for num in arr:
        if num in seen:
            duplicates.add(num)
        else:
            seen.add(num)
    return list(duplicates)
```

Explanation:

- **Original Code:** For each element, the code checks every subsequent element to find duplicates, which leads to a quadratic time complexity.
- **Optimized Code:** We use two sets: one to track the elements we've already seen and another to store duplicates. Since checking membership in a set is O(1) on average, the overall time complexity becomes O(n).

Challenge 122: Refactor Code for Better Readability

Original Solution: The original code has functions to calculate discounts, taxes, and total prices separately. The logic is functional but can be made more modular:

python

```
def calculate_discount(price, discount):
    discounted_price = price - price * (discount / 100)
    if discounted_price < 0:
```

```
        discounted_price = 0
    return discounted_price

def calculate_tax(price, tax_rate):
    return price * (tax_rate / 100)

def calculate_total(price, discount, tax_rate):
    price_after_discount = calculate_discount(price, discount)
    tax = calculate_tax(price_after_discount, tax_rate)
    total_price = price_after_discount + tax
    return total_price

print(calculate_total(100, 20, 8))
```

Refactored Solution: We can simplify the code by combining repetitive logic into a single helper function:

python

```
def apply_percentage(value, percentage):
    return value * (percentage / 100)

def calculate_total(price, discount, tax_rate):
    price_after_discount = price - apply_percentage(price, discount)
    price_after_tax = price_after_discount + apply_percentage(price_after_discount, tax_rate)
    return price_after_tax

print(calculate_total(100, 20, 8))
```

Explanation:

- **Original Code:** We have separate functions for discount and tax calculations, which leads to redundant percentage calculations.
- **Refactored Code:** By abstracting the percentage calculation into the helper function apply_percentage, we reduce redundancy and improve clarity.

DEBUGGING AND OPTIMIZATION

Challenge 123: Improve the Algorithm for Sorting

Original Solution: The original solution uses bubble sort, which is inefficient for larger datasets:

python

```
def bubble_sort(arr):
    for i in range(len(arr)):
        for j in range(0, len(arr) - i - 1):
            if arr[j] > arr[j + 1]:
                arr[j], arr[j + 1] = arr[j + 1], arr[j]
    return arr

print(bubble_sort([64, 34, 25, 12, 22, 11, 90]))
```

Optimized Solution: We can replace bubble sort with a more efficient sorting algorithm such as quicksort or use Python's built-in sorted() function, which uses Timsort with a time complexity of O(n log n):

python

```
def quicksort(arr):
    if len(arr) <= 1:
        return arr
    pivot = arr[0]
    less = [x for x in arr[1:] if x <= pivot]
    greater = [x for x in arr[1:] if x > pivot]
    return quicksort(less) + [pivot] + quicksort(greater)

print(quicksort([64, 34, 25, 12, 22, 11, 90]))
```

Or simply use Python's built-in sorted() function:

python

```
data = [64, 34, 25, 12, 22, 11, 90]
sorted_data = sorted(data)
```

Explanation:

- **Bubble Sort:** Has a time complexity of O(n^2) and performs poorly for large datasets.
- **Quicksort or Sorted():** Both are much more efficient, with a time complexity of O(n log n). Quicksort is a well-known divide-and-conquer algorithm that works by selecting a pivot and sorting the list recursively.

Challenge 124: Optimize a Search Algorithm

Original Solution: The original solution uses linear search, which has a time complexity of O(n):

python

```
def linear_search(arr, target):
    for i in range(len(arr)):
        if arr[i] == target:
            return i
    return -1
```

Optimized Solution: If the list is sorted, we can use binary search, which has a time complexity of O(log n). Here's the binary search implementation:

python

```
def binary_search(arr, target):
    left, right = 0, len(arr) - 1
    while left <= right:
        mid = (left + right) // 2
        if arr[mid] == target:
            return mid
        elif arr[mid] < target:
            left = mid + 1
        else:
```

```
        right = mid - 1
    return -1

arr = [1, 2, 5, 5, 6, 9]
print(binary_search(arr, 9))
```

Explanation:

- **Linear Search:** Has a time complexity of O(n), meaning it scans the entire list to find the target.
- **Binary Search:** Efficiently narrows the search range by half at each step, reducing the time complexity to O(log n), but requires the list to be sorted beforehand.

Challenge 125: Improve Memory Usage in a Function

Original Solution: The original solution stores all squared values in a list, which is memory-intensive for large datasets:

python

```
def generate_squares(n):
    squares = []
    for i in range(n):
        squares.append(i ** 2)
    return squares

print(generate_squares(1000000))
```

Optimized Solution: We can use a generator to yield each squared value one by one, which reduces memory usage significantly:

python

```
def generate_squares(n):
    for i in range(n):
```

```python
        yield i ** 2

squares_generator = generate_squares(1000000)
for square in squares_generator:
    if square > 100:
        break
```

Explanation:

- **Original Code:** Stores all squared values in memory at once, which can be inefficient when dealing with large numbers.
- **Optimized Code:** The generator uses yield to produce values one by one, avoiding the need to store all values in memory simultaneously.

Challenge 126: Refactor a Recursive Function for Efficiency

Original Solution: The original Fibonacci function uses plain recursion, resulting in redundant calculations:

python

```
def fibonacci(n):
    if n <= 1:
        return n
    return fibonacci(n - 1) + fibonacci(n - 2)

print(fibonacci(35))
```

Optimized Solution: We can use memoization to cache previously computed Fibonacci values, improving the performance to O(n):

python

```
def fibonacci(n, memo={}):
    if n <= 1:
        return n
```

```
    if n not in memo:
        memo[n] = fibonacci(n - 1, memo) + fibonacci(n - 2, memo)
    return memo[n]

print(fibonacci(35))
```

Explanation:

- **Original Code:** The recursive calls result in recalculating the same Fibonacci numbers multiple times, leading to exponential time complexity.
- **Optimized Code:** Memoization stores the results of previous calculations in a dictionary, eliminating redundant work and improving the time complexity to O(n).

Challenge 127: Simplify a Complex Expression

Original Solution: The original function calculates the price with discount and tax in a complex expression:

python

```
def calculate_price(price, discount, tax):
    return (price - price * (discount / 100)) * (1 + (tax / 100))
```

Refactored Solution: We can break the expression into smaller parts for readability and clarity:

python

```
def calculate_price(price, discount, tax):
    price_after_discount = price - (price * (discount / 100))
    total_price = price_after_discount * (1 + (tax / 100))
    return total_price
```

Explanation:

- **Original Code:** The expression is concise but can be difficult to understand and debug.
- **Refactored Code:** By splitting the logic into distinct steps, the code becomes easier to follow and debug.

Challenge 128: Reduce Redundant Calculations

Original Solution: The original solution calculates the area and circumference of a circle in separate functions, leading to redundant calculations:

python

```
def calculate_area(radius):
    return 3.14159 * radius ** 2

def calculate_circumference(radius):
    return 2 * 3.14159 * radius

def calculate(radius):
    area = calculate_area(radius)
    circumference = calculate_circumference(radius)
    return area, circumference

print(calculate(5))
```

Optimized Solution: We can calculate both area and circumference in a single function to avoid redundancy:

python

```
def calculate(radius):
    pi = 3.14159
    area = pi * radius ** 2
    circumference = 2 * pi * radius
    return area, circumference

print(calculate(5))
```

Explanation:

- **Original Code:** The constant 3.14159 is calculated twice.
- **Optimized Code:** We calculate pi once and use it for both area and circumference calculations, improving efficiency.

By applying these optimization strategies, we not only improve code efficiency but also enhance readability, memory usage, and algorithmic complexity, making our code more effective in handling larger datasets or more complex tasks.

Test Your Knowledge: Quiz on Debugging and Optimization

Test your understanding of debugging and optimization concepts with the following quiz. These questions will help solidify your knowledge of common errors, debugging techniques, and strategies for optimizing your code. After completing the quiz, check your answers to assess how well you have grasped these critical aspects of programming.

1. What is the primary difference between a syntax error and a logic error?

a) A syntax error occurs when the code violates Python's grammar, while a logic error occurs when the code runs but produces incorrect results.

b) A syntax error causes the program to crash, while a logic error does not.

c) A logic error occurs when there is a typo in the code, while a syntax error causes the program to run incorrectly.

d) There is no difference between syntax errors and logic errors.

2. Which of the following is an example of a time complexity of $O(n^2)$?

a) Binary search on a sorted list

b) A loop inside another loop

c) Sorting a list using quicksort

d) Calculating the sum of elements in a list

3. What does memoization do in recursive functions?
a) It stores function results in a cache to avoid redundant calculations.
b) It changes the structure of recursive calls to be iterative.
c) It reduces the number of recursive calls.
d) It optimizes the space complexity of recursive functions.

4. In Python, which of the following data structures is most efficient for looking up if an element exists, in terms of time complexity?
a) List
b) Set
c) Tuple
d) Dictionary

5. What would be the best way to optimize a function that iterates through a large list to check for duplicates?
a) Use a nested loop to compare every element to every other element.
b) Use a set to track seen elements, reducing time complexity to O(n).
c) Use a dictionary to store the elements and their indices.
d) Sort the list before performing the comparison.

6. What is the time complexity of the bubble sort algorithm?
a) O(n log n)
b) O(n)
c) O(n^2)
d) O(log n)

7. Which of the following optimizations would most likely improve the efficiency of a recursive function?
a) Convert the recursion into a while loop.
b) Use a global variable instead of passing arguments.
c) Apply memoization to store intermediate results.

d) Reduce the number of loops in the code.

8. How can you debug a Python program that runs without errors but does not produce the expected results?

a) Use print() statements to check the values of variables at different points in the program.

b) Try running the program in a different programming language.

c) Rewrite the program from scratch.

d) Ignore the issue, as the program doesn't have any errors.

9. What is the most efficient way to search for an element in a sorted list?

a) Linear search
b) Binary search
c) Bubble sort
d) Hashing

10. In terms of memory usage, which approach is more efficient when dealing with large datasets:

a) Storing all data in a list
b) Using a generator function that yields data one element at a time
c) Using recursion instead of loops
d) Using multiple nested loops to process all data at once

11. Which of the following is the primary advantage of using a generator over a list?

a) Generators use more memory than lists.

b) Generators allow for lazy evaluation, meaning data is produced only when needed.

c) Lists are always faster than generators.

d) Generators cannot be iterated multiple times.

12. When optimizing code for time complexity, what is the focus?

a) Reducing the number of lines of code.
b) Minimizing the number of function calls.
c) Reducing the number of iterations or recursive calls.
d) Making the code run on the fastest hardware.

13. What does the yield keyword do in Python?
a) It terminates the function immediately and returns a value.
b) It causes the function to run faster.
c) It allows the function to return a value and then resume execution later.
d) It makes the function run as a background task.

14. Which of the following algorithms is the most efficient for sorting large datasets?
a) Selection sort
b) Quick sort
c) Bubble sort
d) Insertion sort

15. How would you improve the performance of a function that performs multiple calculations on a list of large numbers?
a) Use a loop instead of recursion.
b) Optimize the mathematical formulas used in the calculations.
c) Break the function into smaller parts and apply memoization.
d) Use a more efficient data structure, such as a set, to store the results.

Answers:

1. **a** – A syntax error occurs when the code does not follow Python's syntax rules, whereas a logic error happens when the code runs but does not do what is expected.
2. **b** – A nested loop is an example of an O(n^2) time complexity, where n is the size of the input.
3. **a** – Memoization stores results of function calls to prevent redundant

computations.
4. **b** – Sets provide O(1) average time complexity for membership checking.
5. **b** – Using a set is the best approach to reduce the time complexity of finding duplicates from O(n^2) to O(n).
6. **c** – Bubble sort has a time complexity of O(n^2).
7. **c** – Memoization stores previously computed results, optimizing recursion by avoiding repeated calculations.
8. **a** – print() statements or using a debugger can help trace the program's state and identify why it's not behaving as expected.
9. **b** – Binary search is the most efficient method for searching in a sorted list, with a time complexity of O(log n).
10. **b** – Using a generator function is more memory efficient for large datasets as it generates data one item at a time.
11. **b** – Generators allow lazy evaluation, meaning data is only computed when needed, which is more memory efficient than storing everything in a list.
12. **c** – Time complexity optimization focuses on reducing the number of iterations or recursive calls required to solve the problem.
13. **c** – The yield keyword allows a function to return a value and pause its execution, resuming later.
14. **b** – Quick sort is typically the most efficient algorithm for sorting large datasets with an average time complexity of O(n log n).
15. **c** – Breaking the function into smaller parts and applying memoization helps improve performance, especially for large datasets with repeated calculations.

Review and Apply:

Take the quiz again after practicing the techniques in this chapter to assess your improvement. Debugging and optimization are ongoing processes, and the more problems you solve, the better you'll become at recognizing opportunities for improvement in your code.

Object-Oriented Programming Essentials

Overview: Why and How to Use OOP in Python

Object-Oriented Programming (OOP) is a programming paradigm that uses the concept of "objects" to design and structure software. In Python, OOP is a fundamental programming technique that allows developers to write code that is modular, reusable, and more maintainable. Understanding the principles of OOP and how to apply them effectively in Python will help you create more organized, scalable, and flexible programs.

Why Use OOP in Python?
Modularity and Reusability

- OOP allows you to break down complex problems into smaller, manageable components (objects). Each object is a self-contained unit that performs a specific task. By organizing your code into classes and objects, you can reuse them in different parts of the program or even in different projects. This modularity reduces the need to write repetitive code and makes maintenance easier.

Maintainability

- Since OOP organizes code into classes and objects, it makes it easier to understand, modify, and extend. When new requirements are introduced, you can add new classes or modify existing ones without affecting other parts of the program. This is particularly important in large applications, where changes are frequent.

Abstraction and Encapsulation

- OOP allows you to hide the internal workings of an object from the outside world through abstraction. By using classes and methods, you can expose only the necessary details, keeping the implementation hidden. This makes it easier for developers to interact with objects without worrying about how they work internally. Encapsulation, another OOP principle, bundles data and the methods that operate on that data into a single unit, ensuring that data is protected and can only be accessed through specified methods.

Inheritance and Code Sharing

- One of the key features of OOP is inheritance, which allows a class to inherit properties and behaviors (methods) from another class. This enables you to create hierarchical relationships between classes, promoting code reuse and reducing redundancy. For example, a child class can extend or modify the functionality of a parent class without needing to rewrite the code.

Polymorphism

- Polymorphism allows objects of different classes to be treated as instances of the same class through a common interface. This makes it possible to write more flexible and generic code. For example, a method in a base class can be overridden in a derived class to provide specialized behavior, while still maintaining the same interface.

Real-world Modeling

- OOP helps to model real-world entities and interactions more intuitively. You can think of objects as real-world entities that have attributes (properties) and behaviors (methods). This mapping between real-world concepts and programming constructs makes it easier to design systems that are closer to how we perceive the world.

Scalability

- As projects grow in complexity, OOP provides a way to manage that growth. By breaking down a problem into smaller classes, you can build a scalable and adaptable system. OOP allows teams to work in parallel on different parts of a system without interfering with each other, making it ideal for large-scale applications.

How to Use OOP in Python

To understand how to implement OOP in Python, let's first define the core concepts:

Classes and Objects

- A class is a blueprint for creating objects (instances), providing initial values for state (variables) and behavior (methods). An object is an instance of a class.

Here's a simple example:

```python
class Dog:
    # Constructor method (initializer)
    def __init__(self, name, breed):
        self.name = name  # Instance variable
```

OBJECT-ORIENTED PROGRAMMING ESSENTIALS

```python
        self.breed = breed  # Instance variable

    # Method to simulate barking
    def bark(self):
        print(f"{self.name} says Woof!")

# Creating an object (instance) of the class Dog
dog1 = Dog("Buddy", "Golden Retriever")
dog1.bark()  # Output: Buddy says Woof!
```

In the example above:

- Dog is a class with a constructor (__init__) that initializes the name and breed attributes for the objects.
- The bark() method defines the behavior of the dog object.
- dog1 is an instance (object) of the Dog class.

Constructor Method: __init__

- The __init__ method is a special method in Python classes. It is used to initialize the state of an object when it is created. This method is automatically called when an object is instantiated from a class. You can pass parameters to __init__ to initialize specific attributes of the object.

Instance Variables and Methods

- **Instance variables** are specific to each object. These variables hold data that describes the state of an object. Instance variables are defined using self, which refers to the current object.
- **Methods** are functions that are defined inside a class and describe the behavior of the objects. Methods also take self as the first parameter, which refers to the instance of the class.

Accessing Attributes and Methods

- You can access an object's attributes and methods using the dot notation:

```python
dog1.name   # Accessing the name attribute
dog1.bark() # Calling the bark method
```

Inheritance

- Inheritance allows one class to inherit attributes and methods from another class. This promotes code reuse. The class inheriting from another class is called the **child class**, and the class being inherited from is called the **parent class**.

Example:

```python
class Animal:
    def __init__(self, name):
        self.name = name

    def speak(self):
        print(f"{self.name} makes a sound.")

class Dog(Animal):
    def speak(self):
        print(f"{self.name} barks!")

# Creating an object of the Dog class
dog = Dog("Max")
dog.speak()  # Output: Max barks!
```

OBJECT-ORIENTED PROGRAMMING ESSENTIALS

In this example:

- Dog inherits from Animal.
- The speak() method in Dog overrides the method in Animal to provide specialized behavior.

Polymorphism

- Polymorphism allows methods to have different behaviors depending on the object that is calling them. A subclass can override methods in its parent class, but you can still call the method using the parent class reference.

Example:

```python
class Cat(Animal):
    def speak(self):
        print(f"{self.name} meows!")

# Polymorphism in action
animals = [Dog("Buddy"), Cat("Whiskers")]

for animal in animals:
    animal.speak()
# Output:
# Buddy barks!
# Whiskers meows!
```

Encapsulation

- Encapsulation refers to the bundling of data (attributes) and methods (functions) within a class. It hides the internal state of the object and only exposes necessary functionality to the outside world. In Python, you can use underscores to indicate that a variable or method should

not be accessed directly from outside the class.
- **Public attributes:** Accessible from outside the class.
- **Private attributes:** Denoted by a double underscore __, these are intended to be inaccessible directly from outside the class.

Abstraction

- Abstraction involves hiding complex implementation details and exposing only essential functionality. In Python, abstraction can be achieved through abstract base classes (ABCs) and interfaces.
- Abstract methods are declared in abstract classes, which cannot be instantiated directly. Instead, subclasses must implement the abstract methods.

1. Example:

python

```
from abc import ABC, abstractmethod

class Animal(ABC):
    @abstractmethod
    def speak(self):
        pass

class Dog(Animal):
    def speak(self):
        print("Woof!")

# animal = Animal()  # This will raise an error because you
cannot instantiate an abstract class
dog = Dog()
dog.speak()  # Output: Woof!
```

OBJECT-ORIENTED PROGRAMMING ESSENTIALS

Object-Oriented Programming is a powerful paradigm that helps create well-structured and maintainable Python code. It promotes modularity, reusability, and flexibility, which are crucial for building scalable applications. By understanding and applying the principles of OOP, you can write Python programs that are easier to read, extend, and debug. Whether you're building a small script or a large software project, OOP is an essential tool in your programming toolkit.

Challenge 131–140: Basic Object-Oriented Concepts

Topics: Classes, Objects, Attributes, Methods

In these challenges, we'll dive into the fundamentals of Object-Oriented Programming (OOP) in Python. These exercises will give you hands-on experience with the basic OOP concepts such as **classes**, **objects**, **attributes**, and **methods**. By the end of this section, you will be comfortable creating simple classes, defining attributes, and understanding the core structure of objects.

Challenge 131: Define a Simple Class

Objective: Create a basic class that represents a real-world entity.
Instructions:

- Define a class called Car.
- The class should have two attributes: make (a string) and year (an integer).
- Create an instance of this class and print its attributes.

Solution:

```python
class Car:
    def __init__(self, make, year):
        self.make = make
```

```
        self.year = year

# Creating an object of the Car class
car1 = Car("Toyota", 2020)
print(f"Car Make: {car1.make}, Year: {car1.year}")
```

Explanation:

- The class Car has two attributes: make and year, initialized in the __init__ constructor.
- An instance car1 is created with the values "Toyota" and 2020 for make and year, respectively.
- The attributes are accessed using dot notation and printed.

Challenge 132: Add a Method to the Class

Objective: Add a method to the Car class that displays the car's full description.

Instructions:

- Define a method inside the Car class called get_car_description().
- The method should return a string that combines the make and year attributes.

Solution:

```python
class Car:
    def __init__(self, make, year):
        self.make = make
        self.year = year

    def get_car_description(self):
        return f"{self.year} {self.make}"
```

```python
# Creating an object of the Car class
car1 = Car("Honda", 2022)
print(car1.get_car_description())  # Output: 2022 Honda
```

Explanation:

- The get_car_description method returns a string that combines the year and make of the car.
- The method is called on the car1 object to get its description.

Challenge 133: Modify Attributes After Object Creation
Objective: Modify the attributes of an existing object.
Instructions:

- After creating an instance of the Car class, change the make and year attributes.
- Print the modified attributes.

Solution:

```python
class Car:
    def __init__(self, make, year):
        self.make = make
        self.year = year

# Creating an object of the Car class
car1 = Car("Ford", 2021)

# Modifying the attributes
car1.make = "Chevrolet"
car1.year = 2023
```

```
print(f"Updated Car Make: {car1.make}, Year: {car1.year}")
```

Explanation:

- The make and year attributes are updated directly after the object car1 is created.
- The modified values are printed out.

Challenge 134: Create Multiple Objects
Objective: Create multiple instances of the same class.
Instructions:

- Define the Car class as before.
- Create three instances of the Car class with different values for make and year.
- Print the details for each object.

Solution:

```python
class Car:
    def __init__(self, make, year):
        self.make = make
        self.year = year

# Creating multiple objects
car1 = Car("Tesla", 2022)
car2 = Car("Ford", 2021)
car3 = Car("BMW", 2023)

# Printing details of each car
print(car1.get_car_description())  # Output: 2022 Tesla
print(car2.get_car_description())  # Output: 2021 Ford
print(car3.get_car_description())  # Output: 2023 BMW
```

OBJECT-ORIENTED PROGRAMMING ESSENTIALS

Explanation:

- Three Car objects (car1, car2, and car3) are created with different make and year values.
- Each object's method get_car_description is called to print their details.

Challenge 135: Working with Class Attributes

Objective: Understand the difference between instance and class attributes.

Instructions:

- Define a class Student with a class attribute school_name.
- Each student object should have an instance attribute name and grade.
- Print the school_name using both class and instance references.

Solution:

```python
class Student:
    school_name = "Greenwood High"

    def __init__(self, name, grade):
        self.name = name
        self.grade = grade

# Creating an object of the Student class
student1 = Student("Alice", "A")
student2 = Student("Bob", "B")

# Accessing the class attribute
print(f"School Name (via class): {Student.school_name}")

# Accessing the class attribute via the object
print(f"School Name (via object): {student1.school_name}")
```

```python
# Accessing instance attributes
print(f"Student 1: {student1.name}, Grade: {student1.grade}")
print(f"Student 2: {student2.name}, Grade: {student2.grade}")
```

Explanation:

- school_name is a class attribute, shared by all instances of the Student class.
- Both class and instance references can access school_name, but the class reference is generally preferred for class attributes.
- name and grade are instance attributes, unique to each object.

Challenge 136: Use of self Keyword

Objective: Understand the role of self in instance methods.

Instructions:

- Create a class called Rectangle.
- Define methods to calculate the area and perimeter of the rectangle.
- The class should take length and width as instance attributes.

Solution:

python

```
class Rectangle:
    def __init__(self, length, width):
        self.length = length
        self.width = width

    def area(self):
        return self.length * self.width

    def perimeter(self):
        return 2 * (self.length + self.width)
```

```
# Creating an object of the Rectangle class
rect = Rectangle(5, 3)

print(f"Area: {rect.area()}")         # Output: 15
print(f"Perimeter: {rect.perimeter()}")  # Output: 16
```

Explanation:

- The self parameter in the __init__, area(), and perimeter() methods refers to the current object.
- The area is calculated as the product of length and width, while the perimeter is the sum of all sides.

Challenge 137: Implementing __str__ for String Representation

Objective: Customize the string representation of an object.

Instructions:

- Define a Book class with attributes title and author.
- Implement the __str__ method to return a readable string when an object of the Book class is printed.

Solution:

```python
class Book:
    def __init__(self, title, author):
        self.title = title
        self.author = author

    def __str__(self):
        return f"'{self.title}' by {self.author}"

# Creating an object of the Book class
```

```
book1 = Book("1984", "George Orwell")

# Printing the book details using __str__
print(book1)  # Output: '1984' by George Orwell
```

Explanation:

- The __str__ method is used to define a custom string representation of the object.
- When you print an object, Python automatically calls the __str__ method to convert the object to a string.

Challenge 138: Method Overloading (Simulating in Python)

Objective: Simulate method overloading in Python.

Instructions:

- Create a Rectangle class.
- Define a method set_dimensions() that can accept either two parameters (length and width) or a single parameter (for a square).
- Ensure the method behaves appropriately for both cases.

Solution:

```python
class Rectangle:
    def __init__(self):
        self.length = 0
        self.width = 0

    def set_dimensions(self, length, width=None):
        if width is None:  # Case when it's a square
            self.length = length
            self.width = length
```

OBJECT-ORIENTED PROGRAMMING ESSENTIALS

```
        else:    # Case when it's a rectangle
            self.length = length
            self.width = width

    def area(self):
        return self.length * self.width

# Creating a rectangle and a square
rect = Rectangle()
rect.set_dimensions(5, 3)
print(f"Rectangle Area: {rect.area()}")    # Output: 15

square = Rectangle()
square.set_dimensions(4)
print(f"Square Area: {square.area()}")    # Output: 16
```

Explanation:

- Python does not support traditional method overloading like other languages (e.g., Java). However, you can simulate overloading by checking the number of arguments passed to a method (e.g., using None as a default value for width).
- The set_dimensions() method behaves differently depending on whether one or two parameters are passed.

Challenge 139: Encapsulation in OOP
Objective: Understand the importance of encapsulation.
Instructions:

- Create a Person class with private attributes (__name and __age).
- Add getter and setter methods to access and modify these private attributes.

Solution:

```python
class Person:
    def __init__(self, name, age):
        self.__name = name
        self.__age = age

    def get_name(self):
        return self.__name

    def set_name(self, name):
        self.__name = name

    def get_age(self):
        return self.__age

    def set_age(self, age):
        self.__age = age

# Creating a person object
person1 = Person("Alice", 30)

# Accessing attributes through getter and setter methods
print(person1.get_name())   # Output: Alice
person1.set_age(31)
print(person1.get_age())    # Output: 31
```

Explanation:

- The __name and __age attributes are encapsulated (private) by prefixing them with __.
- The getter and setter methods are used to safely access and modify the private attributes.

Challenge 140: Polymorphism Example with Shapes
Objective: Understand polymorphism by simulating different shapes.
Instructions:

OBJECT-ORIENTED PROGRAMMING ESSENTIALS

- Create a base class Shape with an abstract method area().
- Derive two classes Circle and Rectangle from Shape, and implement the area() method for both classes.
- Demonstrate polymorphism by calling area() on instances of both classes.

Solution:

```python
import math

class Shape:
    def area(self):
        pass

class Circle(Shape):
    def __init__(self, radius):
        self.radius = radius

    def area(self):
        return math.pi * self.radius ** 2

class Rectangle(Shape):
    def __init__(self, length, width):
        self.length = length
        self.width = width

    def area(self):
        return self.length * self.width

# Polymorphism in action
shapes = [Circle(5), Rectangle(4, 6)]

for shape in shapes:
    print(f"Area: {shape.area()}")
```

Explanation:

- Shape is a base class with an abstract area() method.
- Both Circle and Rectangle classes override the area() method to implement specific behavior.
- The list shapes contains both Circle and Rectangle objects, and polymorphism allows calling the area() method on both objects without knowing their specific types.

Challenge 141–150: Applying OOP Concepts to Practical Problems

Topics: Inheritance, Encapsulation, Simple OOP Applications

In this section, we will explore more advanced uses of **Object-Oriented Programming (OOP)** concepts, including **inheritance** and **encapsulation**. These challenges will help you build more sophisticated applications and design patterns. By the end of these challenges, you will have a strong understanding of how to implement real-world problems using OOP principles.

Challenge 141: Inheritance and Method Overriding

Objective: Implement inheritance and method overriding.

Instructions:

- Create a base class called Animal with a method make_sound().
- Create two subclasses: Dog and Cat, each of which overrides the make_sound() method to produce their respective sounds ("Bark" for Dog, "Meow" for Cat).
- Instantiate both subclasses and call their methods.

Solution:

```python
class Animal:
    def make_sound(self):
        print("Some animal sound")

class Dog(Animal):
    def make_sound(self):
        print("Bark")

class Cat(Animal):
    def make_sound(self):
        print("Meow")

# Creating instances of Dog and Cat
dog = Dog()
cat = Cat()

# Calling the overridden method
dog.make_sound()    # Output: Bark
cat.make_sound()    # Output: Meow
```

Explanation:

- The Dog and Cat classes inherit from the Animal class.
- Both Dog and Cat override the make_sound() method to provide their specific implementations.
- When the make_sound() method is called on each instance, the overridden version is executed.

Challenge 142: Using super() for Parent Class Methods

Objective: Learn how to call a method from a parent class using the super() function.

Instructions:

- Create a Person class with an __init__ method that initializes name

and age attributes.
- Create a subclass Employee that inherits from Person and adds an employee_id attribute.
- Use super() to initialize the Person attributes in the Employee class.

Solution:

```python
class Person:
    def __init__(self, name, age):
        self.name = name
        self.age = age

class Employee(Person):
    def __init__(self, name, age, employee_id):
        super().__init__(name, age)  # Calling the parent class's __init__ method
        self.employee_id = employee_id

# Creating an Employee object
emp = Employee("Alice", 30, "E123")

print(f"Name: {emp.name}, Age: {emp.age}, Employee ID: {emp.employee_id}")
```

Explanation:

- The Employee class inherits from Person and adds the employee_id attribute.
- The super().__init__(name, age) call ensures that the name and age attributes are initialized via the Person class constructor.

Challenge 143: Encapsulation in Action

Objective: Implement encapsulation to hide data and provide controlled access to it.

Instructions:

- Create a class BankAccount with private attributes balance and owner_name.
- Add getter and setter methods to access and modify the balance.
- Ensure that balance cannot be set to a negative value by the setter.

Solution:

```python
class BankAccount:
    def __init__(self, owner_name, balance):
        self.__owner_name = owner_name
        self.__balance = balance

    def get_balance(self):
        return self.__balance

    def set_balance(self, balance):
        if balance >= 0:
            self.__balance = balance
        else:
            print("Balance cannot be negative.")

# Creating a BankAccount object
account = BankAccount("Alice", 1000)

# Accessing and modifying the balance
print(account.get_balance())    # Output: 1000
account.set_balance(1200)
print(account.get_balance())    # Output: 1200
account.set_balance(-500)       # Output: Balance cannot be
```

negative.

Explanation:

- The BankAccount class uses encapsulation by making the balance and owner_name attributes private (by prefixing them with __).
- The get_balance() method is used to retrieve the balance, and the set_balance() method ensures that the balance cannot be set to a negative value.

Challenge 144: Inheriting from Multiple Classes (Multiple Inheritance)

Objective: Understand and implement multiple inheritance in Python.
Instructions:

- Create two classes: Person (with name and age attributes) and Employee (with employee_id attribute).
- Create a subclass Manager that inherits from both Person and Employee and adds a department attribute.
- Instantiate the Manager class and print all the attributes.

Solution:

```python
class Person:
    def __init__(self, name, age):
        self.name = name
        self.age = age

class Employee:
    def __init__(self, employee_id):
        self.employee_id = employee_id
```

```python
class Manager(Person, Employee):
    def __init__(self, name, age, employee_id, department):
        Person.__init__(self, name, age)
        Employee.__init__(self, employee_id)
        self.department = department

# Creating an instance of Manager
manager = Manager("Alice", 35, "M123", "HR")

print(f"Name: {manager.name}, Age: {manager.age}, Employee ID: {manager.employee_id}, Department: {manager.department}")
```

Explanation:

- The Manager class inherits from both Person and Employee.
- The constructor calls the constructors of both parent classes to initialize their attributes.
- The Manager class adds its own department attribute.

Challenge 145: Polymorphism with Method Overriding

Objective: Implement polymorphism with method overriding.

Instructions:

- Create a Shape class with a method area() that is overridden in subclasses Circle and Rectangle.
- Create a list of Shape objects (with Circle and Rectangle instances) and call the area() method polymorphically.

Solution:

python

```python
import math

class Shape:
    def area(self):
        pass

class Circle(Shape):
    def __init__(self, radius):
        self.radius = radius

    def area(self):
        return math.pi * self.radius ** 2

class Rectangle(Shape):
    def __init__(self, length, width):
        self.length = length
        self.width = width

    def area(self):
        return self.length * self.width

# List of shapes
shapes = [Circle(5), Rectangle(4, 6)]

for shape in shapes:
    print(f"Area: {shape.area()}")
```

Explanation:

- Circle and Rectangle both override the area() method from the Shape class.
- The area() method is called polymorphically on each object in the shapes list, allowing different implementations to be executed depending on the object type.

OBJECT-ORIENTED PROGRAMMING ESSENTIALS

Challenge 146: Static Methods and Class Methods

Objective: Understand the difference between static methods and class methods.

Instructions:

- Create a class Employee with a class method company_name() and a static method is_valid_id().
- The company_name() should return the name of the company, and is_valid_id() should validate if an employee ID contains only alphanumeric characters.

Solution:

```python
class Employee:
    company = "TechCorp"

    def __init__(self, employee_id):
        self.employee_id = employee_id

    @classmethod
    def company_name(cls):
        return cls.company

    @staticmethod
    def is_valid_id(employee_id):
        return employee_id.isalnum()

# Creating an Employee object
emp = Employee("E123")

# Calling class method and static method
print(Employee.company_name())        # Output: TechCorp
print(Employee.is_valid_id("E123"))   # Output: True
print(Employee.is_valid_id("E@123"))  # Output: False
```

Explanation:

- The company_name() method is a class method that operates on the class level (indicated by cls).
- The is_valid_id() method is a static method, which does not depend on the class or instance and operates solely on the provided argument.

Challenge 147: Creating a Real-World Banking System with OOP

Objective: Apply OOP concepts to create a simple banking system.
Instructions:

- Create a BankAccount class with attributes for account_number, account_holder, and balance.
- Add methods for deposit, withdrawal, and viewing balance.
- Use inheritance to create a SavingsAccount class that adds interest calculation.

Solution:

```python
class BankAccount:
    def __init__(self, account_number, account_holder, balance):
        self.account_number = account_number
        self.account_holder = account_holder
        self.balance = balance

    def deposit(self, amount):
        self.balance += amount
        print(f"Deposited {amount}. New balance: {self.balance}")

    def withdraw(self, amount):
        if amount <= self.balance:
            self.balance -= amount
```

```
            print(f"Withdrew {amount}. New balance:
            {self.balance}")
        else:
            print("Insufficient funds.")

    def view_balance(self):
        print(f"Current balance: {self.balance}")

class SavingsAccount(BankAccount):
    def __init__(self, account_number, account_holder, balance,
    interest_rate):
        super().__init__(account_number, account_holder, balance)
        self.interest_rate = interest_rate

    def calculate_interest(self):
        interest = self.balance * self.interest_rate / 100
        return interest

# Creating instances of BankAccount and SavingsAccount
account1 = BankAccount("12345", "Alice", 1000)
account1.deposit(500)
account1.withdraw(200)

savings_account = SavingsAccount("67890", "Bob", 2000, 5)
print(f"Interest earned: {savings_account.calculate_interest()}")
```

Explanation:

- The BankAccount class provides basic deposit, withdrawal, and balance viewing functionality.
- The SavingsAccount class inherits from BankAccount and adds an interest calculation feature.

Challenge 148: Building a Simple Inventory System

Objective: Apply OOP principles to build an inventory management system.

Instructions:

- Create a Product class with attributes for product_name, quantity, and price.
- Create methods for updating the quantity, calculating total value, and printing product details.
- Implement inheritance to create a PerishableProduct subclass that adds an expiration date.

Solution:

python

```
class Product:
    def __init__(self, product_name, quantity, price):
        self.product_name = product_name
        self.quantity = quantity
        self.price = price

    def update_quantity(self, new_quantity):
        self.quantity = new_quantity

    def calculate_total_value(self):
        return self.quantity * self.price

    def display_details(self):
        print(f"Product: {self.product_name}, Quantity: {self.quantity}, Price: {self.price}")

class PerishableProduct(Product):
    def __init__(self, product_name, quantity, price, expiration_date):
        super().__init__(product_name, quantity, price)
        self.expiration_date = expiration_date

    def display_details(self):
        super().display_details()
        print(f"Expiration Date: {self.expiration_date}")

# Creating Product and PerishableProduct instances
```

```python
product = Product("Laptop", 10, 999.99)
product.display_details()
print(f"Total Value: {product.calculate_total_value()}")

perishable_product = PerishableProduct("Milk", 30, 2.99, "2024-12-31")
perishable_product.display_details()
```

Explanation:

- The Product class handles basic inventory operations like updating quantity and calculating total value.
- The PerishableProduct subclass adds expiration date functionality and overrides the display_details() method to include this additional information.

Challenge 149: Using OOP to Simulate a Library System

Objective: Implement OOP concepts in a real-world library system.
Instructions:

- Create a Book class with attributes for title, author, and availability.
- Create a Library class that contains a list of books and allows borrowing and returning books.
- Implement methods to search for books by title and author.

Solution:

```python
class Book:
    def __init__(self, title, author, availability=True):
        self.title = title
        self.author = author
```

```python
            self.availability = availability

    def borrow(self):
        if self.availability:
            self.availability = False
            print(f"{self.title} borrowed.")
        else:
            print(f"{self.title} is currently unavailable.")

    def return_book(self):
        self.availability = True
        print(f"{self.title} returned.")

class Library:
    def __init__(self):
        self.books = []

    def add_book(self, book):
        self.books.append(book)

    def search_by_title(self, title):
        for book in self.books:
            if book.title.lower() == title.lower():
                return book
        return None

    def search_by_author(self, author):
        for book in self.books:
            if book.author.lower() == author.lower():
                return book
        return None

# Creating a Library and adding books
library = Library()
book1 = Book("The Great Gatsby", "F. Scott Fitzgerald")
book2 = Book("1984", "George Orwell")
library.add_book(book1)
library.add_book(book2)

# Searching and borrowing books
```

```python
found_book = library.search_by_title("1984")
if found_book:
    found_book.borrow()

found_book = library.search_by_author("F. Scott Fitzgerald")
if found_book:
    found_book.return_book()
```

Explanation:

- The Book class manages attributes like title, author, and availability, along with methods to borrow and return books.
- The Library class contains a list of Book objects and provides methods to search by title and author.

Challenge 150: Building a Simple Chat Application Using OOP

Objective: Build a simple chat system using OOP concepts.

Instructions:

- Create a User class with attributes for username and a list of messages.
- Implement methods to send and receive messages.
- Create a ChatRoom class to manage multiple users and allow users to send messages to each other.

Solution:

```python
class User:
    def __init__(self, username):
        self.username = username
        self.messages = []
```

```python
    def send_message(self, chat_room, message):
        chat_room.broadcast(self, message)

    def receive_message(self, message):
        self.messages.append(message)

    def display_messages(self):
        for msg in self.messages:
            print(f"{self.username}: {msg}")

class ChatRoom:
    def __init__(self):
        self.users = []

    def add_user(self, user):
        self.users.append(user)

    def broadcast(self, sender, message):
        for user in self.users:
            if user != sender:
                user.receive_message(f"{sender.username}: {message}")

# Creating users and a chat room
user1 = User("Alice")
user2 = User("Bob")
user3 = User("Charlie")

chat_room = ChatRoom()
chat_room.add_user(user1)
chat_room.add_user(user2)
chat_room.add_user(user3)

# Sending and receiving messages
user1.send_message(chat_room, "Hello, everyone!")
user2.send_message(chat_room, "Hi Alice, how are you?")
user3.send_message(chat_room, "Hello Alice and Bob!")

# Displaying received messages
user1.display_messages()
```

```
user2.display_messages()
user3.display_messages()
```

Explanation:

- The User class represents a user with a username and a list of messages.
- The ChatRoom class manages multiple users and broadcasts messages to all users except the sender.
- Each user can send messages to the chat room, and receive messages from other users.

These challenges will help solidify your understanding of key OOP principles like inheritance, encapsulation, polymorphism, and method overriding. By solving them, you'll gain hands-on experience in building real-world applications that rely on clean, modular, and reusable code.

Solutions and Explanations (Continued)
Challenge 141: Inheritance and Method Overriding

Solution Explanation: In this challenge, we created a base class Animal with a generic make_sound() method. The Dog and Cat subclasses inherit from Animal and provide their own implementations of make_sound() using method overriding. When we call make_sound() on instances of Dog and Cat, the appropriate method is executed, showcasing polymorphism through method overriding.

- **Inheritance** allows the child classes to inherit attributes and methods from the parent class.
- **Method Overriding** allows child classes to provide a specific implementation of a method that is already defined in the parent class.

Challenge 142: Using super() for Parent Class Methods

Solution Explanation: Here, we used the super() function to call the parent class's __init__ method to initialize attributes name and age in the Employee class. By using super(), we ensure that the Employee class leverages the functionality of its parent class (Person) while adding its own specific behavior, such as initializing the employee_id attribute.

- **super()** helps you call the parent class's method without explicitly naming the parent class, making the code easier to maintain and extend.

Challenge 143: Encapsulation in Action

Solution Explanation: In this challenge, we used **encapsulation** to make the balance and owner_name attributes private (denoted by __). We then provided **getter** (get_balance()) and **setter** (set_balance()) methods to access and modify the balance, while ensuring that negative balances couldn't be set using the setter method.

- **Encapsulation** hides the internal workings of an object and allows controlled access to its attributes.
- **Getter and Setter Methods** allow us to control how we access and modify private attributes.

Challenge 144: Inheriting from Multiple Classes (Multiple Inheritance)

Solution Explanation: Here, the Manager class inherits from both Person and Employee. This is a classic example of **multiple inheritance**, where a class can inherit from more than one class. In the constructor of Manager, we explicitly call the __init__ methods of both Person and Employee to initialize their respective attributes.

- **Multiple Inheritance** allows a class to inherit features from multiple classes, making it more flexible but potentially introducing complexities like method resolution order (MRO).

Challenge 145: Polymorphism with Method Overriding

Solution Explanation: In this challenge, we demonstrated **polymor-**

phism using method overriding. Both Circle and Rectangle override the area() method defined in the parent class Shape. We then created a list of Shape objects (which contains both Circle and Rectangle), and used polymorphism to call the area() method on each object, allowing the correct implementation to execute based on the type of the object.

- **Polymorphism** allows us to call the same method on different objects, but the behavior (method) invoked will differ depending on the object's type.

Challenge 146: Static Methods and Class Methods
Solution Explanation: In this challenge, we distinguished between **class methods** and **static methods**:

- The company_name() method is a **class method**, as it is bound to the class rather than an instance. It uses cls to refer to the class itself.
- The is_valid_id() method is a **static method**, which is not tied to the class or instance and can be called without access to any class or instance variables.
- **Class Methods** are used for operations that are related to the class itself.
- **Static Methods** are used for utility functions that do not modify or interact with instance or class-level data.

Challenge 147: Creating a Real-World Banking System with OOP
Solution Explanation: In this example, we demonstrated basic banking operations using OOP. The BankAccount class provides basic functionality to deposit, withdraw, and view the balance. The SavingsAccount class extends BankAccount and adds functionality to calculate interest. By using inheritance, we keep the base functionality (like deposit and withdrawal) in the BankAccount class, while adding more specific behavior (interest calculation) in the SavingsAccount class.

- **Inheritance** allows us to extend and specialize functionality.
- The super() function is used to initialize the parent class's attributes in the SavingsAccount.

Challenge 148: Building a Simple Inventory System

Solution Explanation: In this challenge, we used **inheritance** to extend the functionality of a product management system. The Product class provides basic functionality like updating quantity and calculating the total value. The PerishableProduct subclass extends Product and adds an expiration date.

- **Inheritance** is useful when we want to create specialized versions of a general class.
- By overriding the display_details() method, we added new functionality specific to PerishableProduct.

Challenge 149: Using OOP to Simulate a Library System

Solution Explanation: The Book class manages attributes like title and availability, while the Library class contains a list of Book objects and supports operations like searching and borrowing books. This system demonstrates **composition**, as the Library class contains instances of the Book class, which is a classic example of "has-a" relationship in OOP.

- **Composition** refers to the practice of building complex objects by combining simpler objects.
- The Library class uses **encapsulation** to manage a list of Book objects and provide controlled access to their operations.

Challenge 150: Building a Simple Chat Application Using OOP

Solution Explanation: This challenge demonstrated the use of **OOP** to simulate a chat application. The User class represents each user in the system, while the ChatRoom class manages all users and broadcasts messages between them. This example utilizes **composition** as well, where the ChatRoom has many User objects. Each User can send messages to the ChatRoom, and the ChatRoom broadcasts the messages to all other users.

- **Composition** allows the ChatRoom to maintain and manage multiple User objects.
- **Polymorphism** is used when different users can interact with the chat system through common interfaces (sending and receiving messages).

These solutions reinforce the core concepts of **Object-Oriented Programming**, such as **inheritance, polymorphism, encapsulation**, and **composition**. Each example builds on fundamental OOP principles and demonstrates how they can be applied to real-world problems.

Mini Project 6: "Bank Account Simulator"
Project Overview

In this mini project, we will build a **Bank Account Simulator** using **Object-Oriented Programming (OOP)**. The objective of this project is to practice applying the principles of **encapsulation, inheritance**, and **polymorphism**. We will create multiple classes, each representing different aspects of a bank account system, and we will use them to simulate basic banking operations like creating accounts, depositing money, withdrawing money, and checking balances.

Project Objectives

- **Create a Bank Account class** to represent a basic account with functionality to deposit, withdraw, and check balance.
- **Extend the Bank Account class** to create specific types of accounts, such as **Savings Account** and **Checking Account**, each with additional features.
- **Ensure proper encapsulation** by keeping sensitive data like account balances private.
- **Demonstrate inheritance** by creating subclasses that extend the base

functionality of the Bank Account class.
- **Apply polymorphism** to handle different types of accounts with a common interface for operations.

Step-by-Step Implementation
Step 1: Create the BankAccount Class
The BankAccount class will serve as the base class, containing the core functionality for all accounts.

python

```python
class BankAccount:
    def __init__(self, owner_name, balance=0):
        self.__owner_name = owner_name  # Encapsulation: private attribute
        self.__balance = balance  # Encapsulation: private attribute

    def deposit(self, amount):
        """Deposit money into the account."""
        if amount > 0:
            self.__balance += amount
            print(f"Deposited ${amount}. New balance: ${self.__balance}")
        else:
            print("Deposit amount must be positive.")

    def withdraw(self, amount):
        """Withdraw money from the account."""
        if amount > 0 and amount <= self.__balance:
            self.__balance -= amount
            print(f"Withdrew ${amount}. New balance: ${self.__balance}")
        elif amount > self.__balance:
            print("Insufficient funds.")
        else:
            print("Withdrawal amount must be positive.")
```

```python
    def get_balance(self):
        """Get the current balance of the account."""
        return self.__balance

    def get_owner(self):
        """Get the account owner's name."""
        return self.__owner_name
```

- **Encapsulation**: The __owner_name and __balance attributes are private (denoted by double underscores __) to ensure that they are not directly accessed from outside the class.
- **Methods**: The deposit(), withdraw(), and get_balance() methods provide functionality for manipulating and accessing the account balance.

Step 2: Create the SavingsAccount Class

Now, we will create a SavingsAccount class that extends BankAccount and adds functionality for earning interest.

python

```
class SavingsAccount(BankAccount):
    def __init__(self, owner_name, balance=0,
    interest_rate=0.02):
        super().__init__(owner_name, balance)  # Call the parent
        constructor
        self.__interest_rate = interest_rate  # Interest rate
        for savings account

    def apply_interest(self):
        """Apply interest to the account balance."""
        interest = self.get_balance() * self.__interest_rate
        new_balance = self.get_balance() + interest
        print(f"Interest applied: ${interest}. New balance:
        ${new_balance}")
```

```
        self.deposit(interest)   # Add the interest to the balance
```

- **Inheritance**: The SavingsAccount class inherits from the BankAccount class and adds its own unique behavior (interest application).
- **super()**: The super().__init__(owner_name, balance) call invokes the parent class's constructor to initialize the common attributes like owner_name and balance.

Step 3: Create the CheckingAccount Class

Next, let's create a CheckingAccount class that adds the capability for overdrafts.

python

```python
class CheckingAccount(BankAccount):
    def __init__(self, owner_name, balance=0,
    overdraft_limit=500):
        super().__init__(owner_name, balance)   # Call the parent
        constructor
        self.__overdraft_limit = overdraft_limit   # Overdraft
        limit for checking accounts

    def withdraw(self, amount):
        """Override the withdraw method to allow overdrafts."""
        if amount > 0 and amount <= self.get_balance() +
        self.__overdraft_limit:
            new_balance = self.get_balance() - amount
            print(f"Withdrew ${amount}. New balance:
            ${new_balance}")
            self.deposit(-amount)   # Decrease balance
        else:
            print(f"Insufficient funds. You can withdraw up to
            ${self.get_balance() + self.__overdraft_limit}
            including overdraft.")
```

OBJECT-ORIENTED PROGRAMMING ESSENTIALS

- **Overriding Methods**: The withdraw() method in CheckingAccount is overridden to allow overdrafts, which means the account balance can go below zero within the specified overdraft limit.
- **super()**: The super().__init__(owner_name, balance) initializes the parent class with common attributes.

Step 4: Demonstrate Bank Account Operations

Now that we have defined the necessary classes, let's demonstrate how we can use them to simulate basic banking operations.

python

```
def simulate_bank_account_operations():
    # Create a BankAccount instance
    account1 = BankAccount("Alice", 1000)
    print(f"Account 1 Owner: {account1.get_owner()}, Balance: ${account1.get_balance()}")

    # Deposit money into account1
    account1.deposit(500)

    # Withdraw money from account1
    account1.withdraw(200)

    # Create a SavingsAccount instance
    savings_account = SavingsAccount("Bob", 1500, 0.05)
    print(f"\nSavings Account Owner: {savings_account.get_owner()}, Balance: ${savings_account.get_balance()}")

    # Apply interest to savings_account
    savings_account.apply_interest()

    # Create a CheckingAccount instance
    checking_account = CheckingAccount("Charlie", 200, 300)
    print(f"\nChecking Account Owner: {checking_account.get_owner()}, Balance: ${checking_account.get_balance()}")
```

```
# Withdraw money with overdraft
checking_account.withdraw(450)
checking_account.withdraw(800)  # This should exceed the
overdraft limit

simulate_bank_account_operations()
```

Expected Output:

bash

```
Account 1 Owner: Alice, Balance: $1000
Deposited $500. New balance: $1500
Withdrew $200. New balance: $1300

Savings Account Owner: Bob, Balance: $1500
Interest applied: $75.0. New balance: $1575
Deposited $75.0. New balance: $1575

Checking Account Owner: Charlie, Balance: $200
Withdrew $450. New balance: -$250
Withdrew $800. Insufficient funds. You can withdraw up to $50
including overdraft.
```

Project Explanation

In this project, we used **Object-Oriented Programming principles** to model a simple bank account system. Here's a breakdown of key concepts used:

1. **Encapsulation**: We encapsulated the account balance and owner details within private variables and exposed them via getter and setter methods.
2. **Inheritance**: We created specialized account classes (SavingsAccount and CheckingAccount) that inherited common functionality from the base BankAccount class.
3. **Polymorphism**: The withdraw() method was overridden in the

CheckingAccount class to introduce overdraft functionality, demonstrating polymorphism by changing behavior in a subclass.

This project provides a practical example of how to organize code using OOP concepts while building a realistic system.

Test Your Knowledge: Quiz on OOP Basics

To ensure that you've grasped the key concepts of **Object-Oriented Programming (OOP)**, we've put together a quick quiz. Answer the following questions based on the material covered in this chapter to test your understanding of the fundamentals of OOP in Python.

1. What is the primary benefit of using **Object-Oriented Programming (OOP)**?

- A) It allows for procedural programming in a more flexible way.
- B) It promotes code reuse and modularity through classes and objects.
- C) It makes the code slower.
- D) It requires no methods or functions.

Answer: B) It promotes code reuse and modularity through classes and objects.

2. What does the __init__ method do in Python?

- A) It initializes variables to their default values.
- B) It is used to define attributes for an object and initialize them.
- C) It initializes the object but does not define attributes.
- D) It is used for error handling in the class.

Answer: B) It is used to define attributes for an object and initialize them.

3. Which of the following is true about **inheritance** in Python?

- A) A subclass can inherit methods and attributes from a parent class.
- B) A parent class can inherit methods and attributes from a subclass.
- C) A class can only inherit from one class.
- D) Inheritance is not supported in Python.

Answer: A) A subclass can inherit methods and attributes from a parent class.

4. In the BankAccount class example, how are the balance and owner attributes protected?

- A) They are declared as public variables.
- B) They are declared as private variables using double underscores (__).
- C) They are made constant using the const keyword.
- D) They are protected by getters and setters only.

Answer: B) They are declared as private variables using double underscores (__).

5. What does the super() function do in Python?

- A) It allows a method from the parent class to be called from the child class.
- B) It provides access to all methods in the current class.
- C) It overrides methods in the child class.
- D) It initializes private attributes of a parent class.

Answer: A) It allows a method from the parent class to be called from the child class.

6. Which of the following is a characteristic of **polymorphism** in OOP?

- A) A subclass cannot change the behavior of a parent class.

- B) A subclass can override methods from the parent class to provide a new implementation.
- C) Methods can only have one function signature.
- D) A class cannot have more than one method with the same name.

Answer: B) A subclass can override methods from the parent class to provide a new implementation.

7. How can you prevent access to an attribute directly from outside the class in Python?

- A) By using a private keyword.
- B) By prefixing the attribute name with double underscores (__).
- C) By using a setter method.
- D) By declaring the class as sealed.

Answer: B) By prefixing the attribute name with double underscores (__).

8. What is the primary purpose of the self keyword in Python classes?

- A) It is used to refer to a variable in the global scope.
- B) It is used to refer to the current object instance.
- C) It is used to refer to a method in the class.
- D) It is used to create new instances of a class.

Answer: B) It is used to refer to the current object instance.

9. What is the advantage of using **getter** and **setter** methods in OOP?

- A) They make attributes accessible only within the class.
- B) They allow indirect access to private variables, providing flexibility and control over how values are set or retrieved.
- C) They increase the performance of the class.

- D) They remove the need for functions and methods.

Answer: B) They allow indirect access to private variables, providing flexibility and control over how values are set or retrieved.

10. Which of the following is an example of **encapsulation** in Python?

    - A) The ability to define multiple classes within a single file.
    - B) Restricting access to an attribute and providing public methods to access or modify it.
    - C) Creating a hierarchy of classes using inheritance.
    - D) Allowing different classes to share common methods.

Answer: B) Restricting access to an attribute and providing public methods to access or modify it.

11. What is the output of the following code snippet?

```python
class Animal:
    def speak(self):
        print("Animal speaks")

class Dog(Animal):
    def speak(self):
        print("Dog barks")

dog = Dog()
dog.speak()
```

- A) Animal speaks
- B) Dog barks
- C) Error because speak() is not defined in Dog.

- D) Error because speak() is not defined in Animal.

Answer: B) Dog barks

12. In a Python class, what is the purpose of the __str__ method?

- A) It defines the string representation of an object when it is printed or converted to a string.
- B) It defines the behavior of the object when used in mathematical operations.
- C) It is used to assign default values to object attributes.
- D) It is used to validate the input values for attributes.

Answer: A) It defines the string representation of an object when it is printed or converted to a string.

Congratulations on completing the quiz! Reviewing the answers and understanding why each is correct (or incorrect) will solidify your understanding of **Object-Oriented Programming (OOP)** concepts in Python. As you move forward, try applying these concepts in real-world projects to build your proficiency.

Advanced Topics for Beginners

Overview: Diving into Advanced Yet Accessible Python Features

As you progress beyond the basics of Python, you will inevitably encounter advanced features that can significantly enhance your programming capabilities. While many of these topics are traditionally reserved for more experienced developers, Python is designed with readability and simplicity in mind. As such, it is entirely possible—and often quite rewarding—to explore some advanced topics early in your learning journey. By doing so, you'll gain deeper insights into Python's flexibility and power, which will help you write more efficient, readable, and maintainable code.

In this chapter, we will introduce you to several advanced but accessible Python features. These topics may seem complex at first, but with a structured approach, you'll be able to understand and leverage them to build better programs. From list comprehensions and generators to decorators and context managers, this chapter will expose you to Python's more sophisticated capabilities, each of which is useful in a variety of programming scenarios.

What to Expect from This Chapter

We'll cover the following key topics:

1. **List Comprehensions** – A concise and efficient way to create lists.
2. **Generators and Iterators** – An introduction to lazy evaluation and

memory-efficient loops.
3. **Decorators** – A powerful way to modify the behavior of functions or methods.
4. **Context Managers** – A mechanism to manage resources efficiently, such as files or network connections.
5. **Lambda Functions** – Anonymous functions that can make your code more elegant and concise.
6. **Error Handling Best Practices** – Advanced techniques for handling exceptions effectively.
7. **The Python Standard Library** – An overview of the most useful modules in Python's rich library.

List Comprehensions: Simplifying List Creation

List comprehensions are one of Python's most celebrated features, allowing you to create lists in a concise, readable, and efficient way. This feature minimizes the need for writing verbose for loops and can significantly reduce the number of lines of code.

Syntax of a List Comprehension:

```python
[expression for item in iterable if condition]
```

- **expression**: The result to append to the list for each item.
- **item**: Each element in the iterable (such as a list, tuple, or range).
- **condition**: An optional condition that filters which elements to include.

Example 1: Basic List Comprehension

```python
squares = [x**2 for x in range(10)]
print(squares)  # Output: [0, 1, 4, 9, 16, 25, 36, 49, 64, 81]
```

Example 2: List Comprehension with Condition

```python
even_squares = [x**2 for x in range(10) if x % 2 == 0]
print(even_squares)  # Output: [0, 4, 16, 36, 64]
```

Why Use List Comprehensions?

- They reduce the verbosity of code and improve readability.
- They offer a performance boost compared to regular for loops because they are optimized in C.
- They encourage the use of functional programming paradigms.

Generators and Iterators: Optimizing Memory Usage

Generators are a powerful Python feature that allows you to iterate over large datasets without storing them entirely in memory. Instead of returning a list, a generator yields values one at a time as you iterate through it. This makes generators perfect for processing large files or streams of data that cannot be held in memory.

Creating a Generator: Generators are defined using functions with the yield keyword instead of return.

Example 1: Basic Generator

```python
def count_up_to(limit):
    count = 1
    while count <= limit:
```

ADVANCED TOPICS FOR BEGINNERS

```
        yield count
        count += 1

counter = count_up_to(5)
for num in counter:
    print(num)  # Output: 1, 2, 3, 4, 5
```

Why Use Generators?

- They allow you to process large datasets efficiently by generating values on demand.
- They save memory because they don't require storing all the values at once.
- They are ideal for infinite or very large sequences where storing all values is impractical.

Decorators: Modifying Function Behavior

Decorators are a way to modify or extend the behavior of functions or methods without changing their actual code. They allow you to add functionality to existing functions in a clean and readable way.

Syntax of a Decorator: A decorator is a function that takes another function as an argument, modifies its behavior, and returns a new function.

Example 1: A Simple Decorator

python

```
def my_decorator(func):
    def wrapper():
        print("Before function call")
        func()
        print("After function call")
    return wrapper

@my_decorator
def say_hello():
```

```
    print("Hello!")

say_hello()
# Output:
# Before function call
# Hello!
# After function call
```

Why Use Decorators?

- They promote **code reuse** and **separation of concerns**.
- They allow you to add behavior to functions (such as logging, access control, or caching) in a clean, maintainable way.
- They simplify code by removing repetitive logic from individual functions.

Context Managers: Managing Resources Automatically

Context managers are used to manage external resources (like files, network connections, or database connections) in an efficient manner. They automatically handle setup and teardown operations, ensuring resources are properly cleaned up after use, even in the event of an error.

Using Context Managers with the with Statement:

```python
with open('example.txt', 'r') as file:
    content = file.read()
    print(content)
# No need to explicitly close the file. It's handled automatically.
```

Creating Your Own Context Manager: You can create custom context managers using the __enter__ and __exit__ methods.

Example 2: Custom Context Manager

```python
class my_open:
    def __init__(self, filename, mode):
        self.filename = filename
        self.mode = mode

    def __enter__(self):
        self.file = open(self.filename, self.mode)
        return self.file

    def __exit__(self, exc_type, exc_value, traceback):
        self.file.close()

with my_open('example.txt', 'w') as file:
    file.write("Hello, world!")
```

Why Use Context Managers?

- They automate resource management, reducing the risk of errors (like forgetting to close a file).
- They ensure proper handling of resources, even when exceptions occur during execution.

Lambda Functions: Compact Anonymous Functions

Lambda functions, also known as anonymous functions, are small functions defined with the lambda keyword. They are often used for short, throwaway functions that are required for a specific task and don't need a formal function definition.

Syntax of a Lambda Function:

```python
lambda arguments: expression
```

Example 1: Simple Lambda Function

```python
square = lambda x: x ** 2
print(square(5))   # Output: 25
```

Why Use Lambda Functions?

- They provide a succinct way to define simple functions for one-off operations.
- They are often used in functional programming methods like map(), filter(), and reduce().

Error Handling Best Practices: Advanced Techniques

In Python, errors and exceptions are inevitable, especially in large programs or when interacting with external systems. Proper error handling ensures that your program can recover from errors gracefully and continue functioning.

Advanced error handling techniques include:

- **Custom exceptions**: Defining your own exceptions to handle specific errors.
- **try-except-else-finally blocks**: Using else to handle successful execution and finally for cleanup, whether an error occurred or not.

Example 1: Custom Exception

```python
class NegativeNumberError(Exception):
    pass

def square_root(number):
```

```
    if number < 0:
        raise NegativeNumberError("Cannot calculate square root
            of a negative number")
    return number ** 0.5

try:
    print(square_root(-1))
except NegativeNumberError as e:
    print(e)  # Output: Cannot calculate square root of a
    negative number
```

Why Use Advanced Error Handling?

- It allows you to write more **robust** and **resilient** code.
- It helps you to handle specific types of errors effectively.
- It ensures your code **fails gracefully** when something goes wrong.

The Python Standard Library: Leveraging Built-In Modules

The Python Standard Library is a collection of modules that provide useful functionality for common tasks. From file handling and data serialization to networking and web scraping, the standard library saves you time by offering tools that would otherwise require building from scratch.

Some popular libraries include:

- **os and sys**: For interacting with the operating system and system-level tasks.
- **json and csv**: For working with JSON and CSV data formats.
- **requests**: For making HTTP requests (although external, it's one of the most used libraries in Python).

Example 2: Using the os Module

```python
import os

# Get the current working directory
print(os.getcwd())
```

Why Use the Python Standard Library?

- It provides solutions for common programming problems without the need for third-party libraries.
- It promotes **code efficiency** and **best practices** by offering pre-built solutions.
- It makes your code more **portable** and **maintainable**.

By now, you should have a good understanding of several advanced yet accessible Python features. These tools and techniques will help you write more efficient, elegant, and maintainable code as you tackle real-world problems. As you continue your Python journey, the concepts introduced in this chapter will form the foundation for even more advanced topics and projects.

Challenge 151–160: Basic Recursion and Data Handling

Recursion is a powerful concept in programming where a function calls itself to solve a smaller version of a problem. It is often used for problems that can be broken down into smaller, similar subproblems, such as searching through a tree structure, calculating factorials, or traversing complex datasets. While recursion can seem tricky at first, it's an essential tool that enhances problem-solving in Python and many other programming languages.

In these challenges, we will walk you through simple recursive functions, explore how recursion works, and provide examples of how recursion can be applied to real-world data problems.

Challenge 151: Calculating Factorial Using Recursion

The factorial of a number is the product of all positive integers less than or equal to that number. Factorial is a classic example used to understand recursion. For example, the factorial of 5 (denoted as 5!) is 5 * 4 * 3 * 2 * 1 = 120.

Task: Write a recursive function to calculate the factorial of a number.
Solution:

```python
def factorial(n):
    # Base case: factorial of 0 is 1
    if n == 0:
        return 1
    else:
        # Recursive case: n * factorial of n-1
        return n * factorial(n - 1)

# Testing the function
print(factorial(5))   # Output: 120
```

Explanation:

- The base case for this recursive function is when n is 0, where the factorial is defined to be 1.
- The recursive case involves calling the function with n - 1 and multiplying it by n, gradually reducing the problem until the base case is reached.

Challenge 152: Summing a List of Numbers Using Recursion

Another common recursive problem is calculating the sum of all elements in a list. Instead of using a loop, we can solve this problem recursively by summing the first element and then calling the function with the rest of the list.

Task: Write a recursive function to sum the elements of a list.
Solution:

python

```
def recursive_sum(numbers):
    # Base case: an empty list has a sum of 0
    if not numbers:
        return 0
    else:
        # Recursive case: first element + sum of the rest of the list
        return numbers[0] + recursive_sum(numbers[1:])

# Testing the function
print(recursive_sum([1, 2, 3, 4, 5]))   # Output: 15
```

Explanation:

- The base case is when the list is empty, and we return 0 (since the sum of an empty list is 0).
- In the recursive case, we sum the first element of the list and recursively call the function on the remaining elements of the list.

Challenge 153: Fibonacci Sequence Using Recursion

The Fibonacci sequence is another classic problem often used to illustrate recursion. In this sequence, each number is the sum of the two preceding ones, starting from 0 and 1.

Task: Write a recursive function to find the nth Fibonacci number.
Solution:

python

```
def fibonacci(n):
    # Base cases
```

```
    if n <= 1:
        return n
    else:
        # Recursive case: sum of the previous two Fibonacci
        numbers
        return fibonacci(n - 1) + fibonacci(n - 2)

# Testing the function
print(fibonacci(6))   # Output: 8
```

Explanation:

- The base case is when n is 0 or 1, where the Fibonacci number is n itself.
- In the recursive case, the function calls itself for the two preceding Fibonacci numbers (n-1 and n-2), and adds them together.

Challenge 154: Reverse a String Using Recursion

Reversing a string is a typical problem that can be solved using recursion. The idea is to take the first character of the string, reverse the rest of the string, and concatenate them.

Task: Write a recursive function to reverse a string.

Solution:

python

```
def reverse_string(s):
    # Base case: if the string is empty or has one character,
    return it
    if len(s) <= 1:
        return s
    else:
        # Recursive case: reverse the rest of the string and add
        the first character
        return reverse_string(s[1:]) + s[0]
```

```
# Testing the function
print(reverse_string("Python"))  # Output: nohtyP
```

Explanation:

- The base case is when the string has a length of 1 or is empty, in which case the string is already reversed.
- The recursive case involves reversing the substring (excluding the first character) and appending the first character to the end.

Challenge 155: Check if a String is Palindromic Using Recursion

A palindrome is a word, phrase, or number that reads the same forward and backward (ignoring spaces, punctuation, and capitalization). This problem can be efficiently solved using recursion.

Task: Write a recursive function to check if a string is a palindrome.
Solution:

python

```
def is_palindrome(s):
    # Remove spaces and convert to lowercase for comparison
    s = s.replace(" ", "").lower()

    # Base case: if the string is empty or has one character,
    it's a palindrome
    if len(s) <= 1:
        return True
    elif s[0] == s[-1]:
        # Recursive case: check if the substring without the
        first and last characters is a palindrome
        return is_palindrome(s[1:-1])
    else:
        return False

# Testing the function
```

```
print(is_palindrome("racecar"))  # Output: True
print(is_palindrome("hello"))    # Output: False
```

Explanation:

- First, we normalize the string by removing spaces and converting it to lowercase.
- The base case checks if the string has one or no characters, in which case it is trivially a palindrome.
- In the recursive case, the function compares the first and last characters. If they match, it calls the function on the remaining substring (excluding the first and last characters).

Challenge 156: Finding the Greatest Common Divisor (GCD) Using Recursion

The greatest common divisor (GCD) of two numbers is the largest number that divides both numbers without leaving a remainder. The Euclidean algorithm is an efficient way to find the GCD, and it can be implemented recursively.

Task: Write a recursive function to find the GCD of two numbers.

Solution:

python

```
def gcd(a, b):
    # Base case: when b is 0, GCD is a
    if b == 0:
        return a
    else:
        # Recursive case: GCD of b and the remainder of a
        divided by b
        return gcd(b, a % b)

# Testing the function
print(gcd(56, 98))  # Output: 14
```

Explanation:

- The base case is when b is 0, in which case the GCD is a.
- The recursive case involves finding the GCD of b and the remainder of a divided by b, which follows the Euclidean algorithm.

Challenge 157: Flatten a Nested List Using Recursion

Nested lists are common in Python, and sometimes, it's necessary to flatten a nested list into a single-level list. This can be done using recursion by iterating through the elements and flattening them when encountering sublists.

Task: Write a recursive function to flatten a nested list.

Solution:

python

```python
def flatten(nested_list):
    flat_list = []
    for item in nested_list:
        if isinstance(item, list):
            # Recursive case: flatten the sublist and add the
            items to the flat list
            flat_list.extend(flatten(item))
        else:
            flat_list.append(item)
    return flat_list

# Testing the function
print(flatten([1, [2, 3], 4, [5, [6, 7]]]))  # Output: [1, 2, 3, 4, 5, 6, 7]
```

Explanation:

- The function iterates through each item in the nested list.
- If the item is a sublist, the function recursively flattens it.
- If the item is not a list, it adds it directly to the flat_list.

Challenge 158: Calculate the Power of a Number Using Recursion

The power of a number refers to the result of raising it to a given exponent. For instance, 3^4 means multiplying 3 by itself 4 times (i.e., 3 * 3 * 3 * 3 = 81).

Task: Write a recursive function to calculate the power of a number.
Solution:

python

```
def power(base, exponent):
    # Base case: any number raised to the power of 0 is 1
    if exponent == 0:
        return 1
    else:
        # Recursive case: base * base^(exponent-1)
        return base * power(base, exponent - 1)

# Testing the function
print(power(3, 4))  # Output: 81
```

Explanation:

- The base case is when the exponent is 0, which always results in 1.
- In the recursive case, we multiply the base by the result of calling the function with a decremented exponent.

Challenge 159: Reverse a List Using Recursion

Reversing a list using recursion is a fundamental challenge that demonstrates how recursion can be applied to data structures like lists.

Task: Write a recursive function to reverse a list.
Solution:

python

```
def reverse_list(lst):
    # Base case: if the list is empty or has one item, return
    the list
    if len(lst) <= 1:
        return lst
    else:
        # Recursive case: reverse the rest of the list and add
        the first element to the end
        return reverse_list(lst[1:]) + [lst[0]]

# Testing the function
print(reverse_list([1, 2, 3, 4, 5]))  # Output: [5, 4, 3, 2, 1]
```

Explanation:

- The base case handles the case where the list has one or no elements, returning it as-is.
- In the recursive case, we reverse the rest of the list and add the first element at the end.

Challenge 160: Count the Occurrences of an Element in a List Using Recursion

Counting the number of times an element appears in a list is another common problem that can be solved efficiently with recursion.

Task: Write a recursive function to count the occurrences of a specified element in a list.

Solution:

python

```
def count_occurrences(lst, value):
    # Base case: if the list is empty, return 0
    if not lst:
        return 0
    elif lst[0] == value:
```

```
        # Recursive case: if the first element matches, count it
        and search the rest
        return 1 + count_occurrences(lst[1:], value)
    else:
        # If no match, just continue with the rest of the list
        return count_occurrences(lst[1:], value)

# Testing the function
print(count_occurrences([1, 2, 3, 2, 4, 2], 2))  # Output: 3
```

Explanation:

- The base case handles the situation where the list is empty, returning 0.
- The recursive case checks if the first element matches the target value. If it does, it increments the count and continues searching the rest of the list.

These challenges cover a variety of basic recursive concepts, including how recursion works in Python and how it can be used to solve common problems.

Challenge 161-170: Working with Modules and Packages

In Python, modules and packages are essential for organizing and reusing code. A **module** is a single file that contains Python definitions and statements. A **package** is a collection of modules organized in a directory structure. By leveraging modules and packages, you can keep your code modular, maintainable, and scalable.

In this section, we will walk through various tasks to understand how to use Python's built-in modules, how to create your own modules, and how to effectively organize code into packages.

Challenge 161: Importing Modules

The ability to import and use external libraries is one of Python's key strengths. This allows you to extend your code with functionalities that would otherwise require you to write large portions of code yourself.

Task: Import the built-in math module and use it to calculate the square root and the value of pi.

Solution:

```python
import math

# Calculate the square root of 25
sqrt_value = math.sqrt(25)

# Get the value of pi
pi_value = math.pi

print("Square root of 25:", sqrt_value)  # Output: 5.0
print("Value of pi:", pi_value)          # Output: 3.141592653589793
```

Explanation:

- The math module provides mathematical functions, constants like pi, and more advanced mathematical operations.
- You can use import math to bring the module into your code and then access its functions and constants with math.function_name.

Challenge 162: Using Specific Functions from a Module

Instead of importing the entire module, you can choose to import only specific functions from a module. This can help reduce memory usage when only a few functions are needed.

Task: Import only the sqrt and pi functions from the math module and use them to perform calculations.

Solution:

```python
```

ADVANCED TOPICS FOR BEGINNERS

```
from math import sqrt, pi

# Calculate the square root of 25
sqrt_value = sqrt(25)

# Get the value of pi
pi_value = pi

print("Square root of 25:", sqrt_value)  # Output: 5.0
print("Value of pi:", pi_value)           # Output:
3.141592653589793
```

Explanation:

- The from math import sqrt, pi statement imports just the sqrt function and the pi constant from the math module, making them directly accessible without needing to prefix them with math..

Challenge 163: Aliasing Modules

When importing modules, especially those with long names, it's often useful to alias them. This means giving a module or function a shorthand name so it's easier to use in your code.

Task: Alias the math module as m and use it to calculate the cosine of 0 degrees.

Solution:

```python
import math as m

# Calculate the cosine of 0 radians
cosine_value = m.cos(0)

print("Cosine of 0:", cosine_value)  # Output: 1.0
```

Explanation:

- import math as m gives the math module a shorthand name (m), making it easier to reference in the code.
- We use m.cos(0) to calculate the cosine of 0 radians (which is 1).

Challenge 164: Building Your Own Module

One of the most powerful features of Python is the ability to organize your own code into modules. By doing so, you can reuse code across multiple projects or files without duplicating it.

Task: Create a simple Python module called math_utils.py with a function to calculate the square of a number, and then import and use this function in another script.

Solution:

Create a file named math_utils.py with the following content:

```python
# math_utils.py

def square(number):
    return number ** 2
```

In another Python script, import and use the square function:

```python
from math_utils import square

# Use the square function from the math_utils module
result = square(4)

print("Square of 4:", result)   # Output: 16
```

Explanation:

- math_utils.py defines a simple square function that returns the square of a given number.

- In the second script, we use from math_utils import square to import the square function from the math_utils.py module and then call it.

Challenge 165: Understanding Python Packages

A package is a collection of related modules. Python packages allow you to organize code into directories, making it easier to manage large projects. A package must contain an __init__.py file (which can be empty) to be recognized as a Python package.

Task: Create a package with multiple modules. Create a package named geometry with two modules: circle.py and rectangle.py. Then, use these modules in another script.

Solution:

Create a directory named geometry, and inside it, create two files: circle.py and rectangle.py.

geometry/circle.py:

```python
# circle.py
import math

def area(radius):
    return math.pi * (radius ** 2)
```

geometry/rectangle.py:

```python
# rectangle.py

def area(length, width):
    return length * width
```

In the geometry directory, create an empty __init__.py file to indicate that it's a package.

In another Python script, import and use the functions from the geometry package:

```python
from geometry.circle import area as circle_area
from geometry.rectangle import area as rectangle_area

# Use the functions from the package
circle_result = circle_area(5)
rectangle_result = rectangle_area(4, 6)

print("Area of circle:", circle_result)       # Output: 78.53981633974483
print("Area of rectangle:", rectangle_result) # Output: 24
```

Explanation:

- The geometry package contains two modules: circle.py and rectangle.py, each with an area function.
- The __init__.py file is required to turn the directory into a Python package.
- In the main script, we import the area functions from both modules and use them to calculate areas.

Challenge 166: Using Standard Library Modules (e.g., os, datetime)

Python comes with many useful built-in libraries. The os library helps with interacting with the operating system (e.g., file management), while the datetime module deals with working with dates and times.

Task: Use the os module to get the current working directory and use the datetime module to print the current date and time.

Solution:

```python
import os
import datetime

# Get the current working directory
current_directory = os.getcwd()

# Get the current date and time
current_datetime = datetime.datetime.now()

print("Current working directory:", current_directory)
print("Current date and time:", current_datetime)
```

Explanation:

- os.getcwd() returns the current working directory (the folder where your Python script is located).
- datetime.datetime.now() returns the current date and time.

Challenge 167: Exploring More Standard Libraries (e.g., random, sys)

Python's standard library includes several other modules, such as random for generating random numbers and sys for system-specific parameters and functions.

Task: Use the random module to generate a random number between 1 and 100, and use the sys module to print the Python version you're using.

Solution:

```python
import random
import sys

# Generate a random number between 1 and 100
random_number = random.randint(1, 100)
```

```
# Print the Python version
python_version = sys.version

print("Random number:", random_number)
print("Python version:", python_version)
```

Explanation:

- random.randint(1, 100) generates a random integer between 1 and 100, inclusive.
- sys.version gives you information about the Python version you're running.

Challenge 168: Creating a Simple Package for Reusable Code

Now that you understand modules and packages, it's time to create a simple package for reusable code.

Task: Create a package named utils with a module math_ops.py that includes a function for calculating the factorial of a number. Then, use this package in another script.

Solution:

Create a directory named utils with a module file math_ops.py. utils/math_ops.py:

```python

# math_ops.py

def factorial(n):
    if n == 0:
        return 1
    else:
        return n * factorial(n - 1)
```

In the utils directory, add an empty __init__.py file.

In another Python script, import and use the factorial function:

```python
from utils.math_ops import factorial

# Test the factorial function
result = factorial(5)

print("Factorial of 5:", result)   # Output: 120
```

Explanation:

- math_ops.py contains a factorial function.
- By creating a __init__.py file, we can treat the utils directory as a package and access the factorial function from math_ops.py.

Challenge 169: Handling Missing Modules with try-except

When you attempt to import a module that isn't installed on your system, Python will raise an ImportError. You can handle this gracefully by using a try-except block to catch the error and either provide a fallback solution or prompt the user to install the missing module.

Task: Write a script that attempts to import a module named numpy (if it's installed). If the module is not found, print a message indicating that the module is missing.

Solution:

```python
try:
    import numpy
    print("Numpy module is installed.")
except ImportError:
    print("Numpy module is not installed. Please install it
    using 'pip install numpy'.")
```

Explanation:

- The try block attempts to import the numpy module.
- If the module is not found, Python raises an ImportError, which is caught by the except block, printing a user-friendly message.

Challenge 170: Exploring and Creating Your Own Python Package

Finally, let's explore how to create your own Python package with multiple modules and distribute it. In this challenge, we'll create a package that performs basic arithmetic operations. This package will include two modules: addition.py and multiplication.py.

Task: Create a directory structure for a package named arithmetic with two modules (addition.py and multiplication.py). Then, write a simple script that imports and uses functions from this package.

Solution:

Create a directory called arithmetic with the following structure:

```markdown
arithmetic/
    __init__.py
    addition.py
    multiplication.py
```

Inside addition.py, write the following code:

```python
# addition.py

def add(a, b):
    return a + b
```

Inside multiplication.py, write the following code:

```python
# multiplication.py

def multiply(a, b):
    return a * b
```

Inside __init__.py, leave it empty to mark the directory as a package.

In another Python script, import and use the functions from the arithmetic package:

```python
from arithmetic.addition import add
from arithmetic.multiplication import multiply

# Use the functions from the arithmetic package
sum_result = add(10, 5)
product_result = multiply(3, 7)

print("Sum of 10 and 5:", sum_result)        # Output: 15
print("Product of 3 and 7:", product_result) # Output: 21
```

Explanation:

- addition.py contains a function to add two numbers.
- multiplication.py contains a function to multiply two numbers.
- The __init__.py file marks the directory as a package.
- In the main script, we import the add and multiply functions from their respective modules in the arithmetic package and use them.

These challenges help solidify your understanding of how to import and use Python modules, work with packages, and create reusable code. They also provide a foundation for structuring larger projects and handling missing modules effectively.

Solutions and Explanations

Let's go through the detailed solutions for each challenge presented in the previous section. Understanding these examples will provide a deeper insight into the functionality and behavior of modules, packages, and advanced Python features.

Challenge 161: Importing Python Modules

Task: The goal of this challenge was to explore the use of external modules in Python by importing the math module and utilizing its functions.

Solution Explanation:

```python
import math

# Using the sqrt() function to calculate the square root
number = 16
sqrt_value = math.sqrt(number)
print(f"The square root of {number} is {sqrt_value}")
```

- The import statement is used to load the math module, which contains a collection of mathematical functions.
- We then use math.sqrt() to find the square root of a given number.
- The result is printed out using an f-string to format the output.

What's Happening:

- Python provides built-in modules such as math to simplify coding. The sqrt() function is one of many useful functions in the math library.
- If you wanted to use any other mathematical functions (like sin(), cos(), or tan()), you can simply call them in a similar way.

Challenge 162: Handling ImportError

Task: This challenge focused on handling scenarios where a module is

not installed by using a try-except block.
Solution Explanation:

```python
try:
    import numpy
    print("Numpy module is installed.")
except ImportError:
    print("Numpy module is not installed. Please install it using 'pip install numpy'.")
```

- We attempted to import the numpy module.
- If the module is installed, it will successfully import, and the message "Numpy module is installed." will be printed.
- If the module is not installed, an ImportError is raised, and the except block catches it, printing a message advising the user to install the module.

What's Happening:

- The try-except block is used to handle exceptions in Python. Here, it allows you to manage scenarios where certain modules are unavailable on the system.
- This is a best practice when you want to ensure your code runs smoothly even if dependencies are not met, offering helpful instructions to the user to fix the issue.

Challenge 163: Creating a Python Package

Task: This challenge guided the creation of a custom package with multiple modules. We created a simple package arithmetic with two modules, addition.py and multiplication.py.

Solution Explanation:

Package Structure: The directory structure of the arithmetic package was as follows:

```markdown
arithmetic/
    __init__.py
    addition.py
    multiplication.py
```

addition.py:

```python
# addition.py

def add(a, b):
    return a + b
```

- The add() function takes two numbers as parameters and returns their sum.

multiplication.py:

```python
# multiplication.py

def multiply(a, b):
    return a * b
```

- The multiply() function takes two numbers and returns their product.

Main Script:

```python
from arithmetic.addition import add
from arithmetic.multiplication import multiply

sum_result = add(10, 5)
product_result = multiply(3, 7)

print("Sum of 10 and 5:", sum_result)        # Output: 15
print("Product of 3 and 7:", product_result) # Output: 21
```

- Here, we imported the add() and multiply() functions from the addition and multiplication modules, respectively.
- We then used these functions to perform basic arithmetic operations, displaying the results using print().

What's Happening:

- The directory structure defines the arithmetic package, and the __init__.py file marks it as a package in Python.
- The add() and multiply() functions in addition.py and multiplication.py are separate modules within the package, making the code modular and reusable.
- In the main script, we import the functions using the from ... import ... syntax and use them to perform operations. This structure is perfect for organizing code in larger projects.

Challenge 164: Importing and Using Standard Libraries

Task: This challenge encouraged users to explore the Python Standard Library by importing and using modules such as os and random to solve basic problems.

Solution Explanation:

```python
import os
import random

# Working with the os module to get the current working directory
cwd = os.getcwd()
print(f"Current working directory: {cwd}")

# Working with the random module to generate a random number
between 1 and 100
random_number = random.randint(1, 100)
print(f"Random number between 1 and 100: {random_number}")
```

- The os module provides a way to interact with the operating system. Here, we use os.getcwd() to get the current working directory.
- The random module is used to generate a random number between 1 and 100 using random.randint().
- Both modules are part of Python's Standard Library, which is bundled with Python and requires no additional installation.

What's Happening:

- The os module offers a variety of utilities to interact with the operating system, such as manipulating files and directories. In this case, getcwd() retrieves the current working directory.
- The random module provides functions for generating random numbers, which can be useful in a variety of applications, from simulations to games.

Key Takeaways:

- **Modules and Packages**: Python makes it easy to extend its functionality with external modules. You can use built-in modules like math or

random or create your own packages to organize your code.
- **Error Handling**: The try-except block is a powerful tool for handling exceptions, allowing your program to fail gracefully when an error occurs.
- **Reusability**: By organizing your code into modules and packages, you can reuse and maintain it more effectively, making it easier to scale projects as they grow.

These challenges and solutions should have enhanced your understanding of how Python handles modules and packages, error handling, and the power of Python's Standard Library in everyday programming tasks.

Mini Project 7: "Mini Calendar App"

In this mini project, we will build a simple calendar application in Python that displays the current month and year, and allows the user to select a specific month and year to view the calendar. This project will help reinforce your understanding of using Python's built-in modules like calendar, along with user input handling and basic functions.

Project Objective

- Learn how to use the calendar module to generate calendar outputs.
- Understand user input handling to customize the view of the calendar.
- Practice basic function creation and modularity.

Step 1: Setting Up the Project

We will use Python's built-in calendar module to generate calendar output for a given month and year. This module provides a function month() that prints the calendar for a specific month and year.

Step 2: Importing Required Modules

The first step is to import the necessary modules. We will need calendar for displaying the calendar and datetime to fetch the current date.

```python
import calendar
import datetime
```

Step 3: Displaying the Current Month and Year

Before we proceed to allow the user to select a specific month and year, we will display the calendar for the current month by default.

```python
# Get current date
current_date = datetime.datetime.now()
current_year = current_date.year
current_month = current_date.month

# Display the current month's calendar
print("Current Calendar:")
print(calendar.month(current_year, current_month))
```

- The datetime.datetime.now() function is used to fetch the current date and time.
- We extract the current year and month from the current date using current_date.year and current_date.month.
- The calendar.month() function takes the year and month as arguments and returns the calendar for that month.

Step 4: Creating User Input for Custom Calendar

Next, let's create a simple user interface that will ask the user for a month and a year to display the calendar for that specific month.

```python
```

ADVANCED TOPICS FOR BEGINNERS

```python
def display_calendar(year, month):
    """Displays the calendar for the specified month and year."""
    print(calendar.month(year, month))

def main():
    """Main function to run the Calendar app."""
    # Display current calendar
    print("Welcome to the Mini Calendar App")
    print("1. View current month's calendar")
    print("2. View a specific month and year")

    choice = int(input("Please choose an option (1 or 2): "))

    if choice == 1:
        # Display current month's calendar
        display_calendar(current_year, current_month)
    elif choice == 2:
        # User input for month and year
        month = int(input("Enter the month (1-12): "))
        year = int(input("Enter the year (e.g., 2024): "))
        display_calendar(year, month)
    else:
        print("Invalid choice. Please select either 1 or 2.")
```

In this step:

- The display_calendar() function takes the year and month as parameters and prints the corresponding calendar.
- The main() function guides the user through the app interface. It allows the user to choose whether to view the current month's calendar or input their desired month and year.
- If the user selects option 1, the app shows the calendar for the current month. If option 2 is selected, the user can enter a specific month and year to see that month's calendar.

Step 5: Adding Error Handling

Let's add basic error handling to ensure that the user enters valid data.

For example, the program should handle cases where the user enters invalid month or year values.

```python
def main():
    """Main function to run the Calendar app."""
    print("Welcome to the Mini Calendar App")
    print("1. View current month's calendar")
    print("2. View a specific month and year")

    try:
        choice = int(input("Please choose an option (1 or 2): "))

        if choice == 1:
            # Display current month's calendar
            display_calendar(current_year, current_month)
        elif choice == 2:
            # User input for month and year
            month = int(input("Enter the month (1-12): "))
            year = int(input("Enter the year (e.g., 2024): "))

            if month < 1 or month > 12:
                print("Invalid month! Please enter a number between 1 and 12.")
            else:
                display_calendar(year, month)
        else:
            print("Invalid choice. Please select either 1 or 2.")
    except ValueError:
        print("Invalid input! Please enter valid numbers.")
```

Key Updates:

- A try-except block is used to catch ValueError exceptions in case the user enters non-numeric input.
- Additional checks ensure the month entered is between 1 and 12.

Step 6: Final Touches

The final version of the Mini Calendar App allows the user to view either the current month's calendar or input a specific month and year. Here's the complete code for the project:

```python

import calendar
import datetime

def display_calendar(year, month):
    """Displays the calendar for the specified month and year."""
    print(calendar.month(year, month))

def main():
    """Main function to run the Calendar app."""
    print("Welcome to the Mini Calendar App")
    print("1. View current month's calendar")
    print("2. View a specific month and year")

    try:
        choice = int(input("Please choose an option (1 or 2): "))

        if choice == 1:
            # Display current month's calendar
            current_date = datetime.datetime.now()
            display_calendar(current_date.year,
            current_date.month)
        elif choice == 2:
            # User input for month and year
            month = int(input("Enter the month (1-12): "))
            year = int(input("Enter the year (e.g., 2024): "))

            if month < 1 or month > 12:
                print("Invalid month! Please enter a number
                between 1 and 12.")
            else:
                display_calendar(year, month)
        else:
            print("Invalid choice. Please select either 1 or 2.")
```

```
    except ValueError:
        print("Invalid input! Please enter valid numbers.")

if __name__ == "__main__":
    main()
```

What We've Learned:

- **Using the calendar Module**: The calendar.month(year, month) function is an efficient way to generate and display calendars.
- **User Input**: Handling user input with input() is essential for interactive applications.
- **Error Handling**: Using try-except blocks ensures that invalid inputs don't crash the program and gives users helpful feedback.
- **Modular Design**: By separating concerns into functions (e.g., display_calendar() and main()), the code becomes more organized and reusable.

This mini project not only demonstrates how to use Python's standard libraries but also gives you a hands-on approach to building a useful and interactive app that you can expand upon in the future.

Test Your Knowledge: Quiz on Advanced Python Features

This quiz will help you assess your understanding of the advanced Python features you've learned in this chapter. The questions cover topics such as recursion, modules, packages, and more. Try to answer the questions based on the concepts discussed in the chapter.

1. **Recursion Basics**

What is the main characteristic of a recursive function in Python?
a) It always loops over the entire dataset.
b) It calls itself within its own body to solve smaller sub-problems.
c) It uses a while loop to repeat an operation.

d) It sorts a list before performing any operation.

2. Understanding Recursion
Which of the following is an example of a valid base case for a recursive function?
a) If x == 0 return 1
b) If x == 0 return x
c) If x > 0 return x * 2
d) If x == 0 return 0

3. Working with Modules
How do you import a specific function, add_numbers(), from a Python module math_operations?
a) import add_numbers from math_operations
b) from math_operations import add_numbers
c) import math_operations.add_numbers
d) add_numbers = math_operations()

4. Creating a Module
Which of the following steps is necessary when creating a Python module?
a) Save the Python script with a .py extension.
b) Import it directly in the main script without saving it.
c) Ensure the script contains only functions with no variables.
d) Ensure the script is compiled into a .exe file.

5. Working with Packages
What is the purpose of a __init__.py file in a Python package?
a) It initializes a function call in the package.
b) It allows Python to recognize the folder as a package.
c) It installs external packages for the project.
d) It defines the metadata of the package.

6. Using External Libraries

Which Python module is commonly used to handle JSON data (encoding and decoding)?

a) calendar
b) json
c) os
d) datetime

7. Recursion Example

What will the following recursive function return when called as factorial(5)?

```python
def factorial(n):
    if n == 1:
        return 1
    else:
        return n * factorial(n - 1)
```

a) 120
b) 60
c) 15
d) 5

8. Error Handling in Recursion

Which of the following issues is most likely to cause a RecursionError in Python?

a) A function doesn't return a value.
b) A function calls itself too many times without a proper base case.
c) A function never calls itself.
d) A function has too many parameters.

9. Working with Functions in Modules

What is the correct syntax to use a function named calculate_area() from

a module named geometry?
   a) import geometry.calculate_area()
   b) from geometry import calculate_area
   c) import calculate_area from geometry
   d) geometry.calculate_area()

10. **Optimizing Recursive Functions**
   In recursion, which strategy helps prevent excessive calls and improves efficiency?
   a) Reduce the number of function parameters.
   b) Use memoization or caching techniques to store results.
   c) Replace recursion with while loops.
   d) Increase the depth of recursion.

11. **Using Python's Built-In Modules**
   Which module is used to handle random number generation in Python?
   a) math
   b) random
   c) time
   d) sys

12. **Packages and Distribution**
   If you want to distribute a Python package so that others can easily install it, which tool would you most likely use?
   a) PyInstaller
   b) pip
   c) setuptools
   d) python3

13. **Understanding Recursion**
   What is a key advantage of recursion over iteration for certain problems?
   a) Recursion provides better memory management.
   b) Recursion is usually faster than iteration.

c) Recursion can lead to more elegant and easier-to-understand code for problems like tree traversal.

d) Recursion allows for parallel execution.

14. Error Handling in Modules

When importing a Python module, what happens if the module cannot be found?

a) The program will crash and terminate immediately.

b) Python will raise an ImportError and attempt to continue execution.

c) The module will be automatically created.

d) Python will prompt the user to install the module.

15. Advanced Function Usage

What is the purpose of *args in a function definition?

a) It collects the function's return value into a list.

b) It allows the function to accept a variable number of positional arguments.

c) It makes the function return multiple values.

d) It stores arguments for later use in the program.

Answer Key:

1. **b)** It calls itself within its own body to solve smaller sub-problems.
2. **a)** If x == 0 return 1
3. **b)** from math_operations import add_numbers
4. **a)** Save the Python script with a .py extension.
5. **b)** It allows Python to recognize the folder as a package.
6. **b)** json
7. **a)** 120
8. **b)** A function calls itself too many times without a proper base case.
9. **b)** from geometry import calculate_area
10. **b)** Use memoization or caching techniques to store results.
11. **b)** random

12. **c)** setuptools
13. **c)** Recursion can lead to more elegant and easier-to-understand code for problems like tree traversal.
14. **b)** Python will raise an ImportError and attempt to continue execution.
15. **b)** It allows the function to accept a variable number of positional arguments.

This quiz tests your understanding of advanced Python features, including recursion, modules, and error handling. Review the concepts covered in the chapter to ensure you fully understand these essential Python skills. Try to implement more examples and challenge yourself with different scenarios to reinforce your learning.

Putting It All Together – Projects and Real-World Applications

Overview: Building Confidence with Larger Projects

As you approach the final stage of your Python learning journey, you've amassed a solid understanding of the language's core concepts. However, to truly master Python and gain confidence in your skills, you must apply what you've learned to real-world projects. Larger, more comprehensive projects provide a unique opportunity to deepen your understanding, sharpen your problem-solving abilities, and solidify your coding proficiency.

In this chapter, we will explore how to transition from writing small code snippets to developing full-fledged applications. By integrating everything you've learned so far—control flow, functions, data structures, file handling, object-oriented programming, debugging, optimization, and more—you will be ready to tackle larger, more complex challenges. These projects will not only help you apply your knowledge but also simulate real-world programming tasks that you may encounter in professional environments.

Why Work on Larger Projects?

1. **Real-World Experience**: While small coding challenges help you understand the syntax and concepts, real-world projects provide the experience of tackling problems you'll face in professional development. They teach you how to think critically, handle requirements from stakeholders, and produce software that is both functional and

maintainable.
2. **Problem-Solving Skills**: Working on larger projects enhances your ability to break down complex problems into manageable pieces. The process of dividing a large project into smaller tasks, deciding on the right tools and approaches, and iterating through the solution improves your problem-solving skills.
3. **Confidence Boost**: Completing a larger project will give you a sense of accomplishment and confidence in your abilities. Being able to take a problem from start to finish and seeing the results in action validates your learning and shows that you can apply it in a real-world setting.
4. **Portfolio Development**: Every project you work on can become part of your coding portfolio. Building a diverse set of projects will showcase your skills to potential employers or collaborators. It gives you concrete examples of what you can do, making you a more attractive candidate for professional roles.
5. **Learning Best Practices**: Developing larger projects helps you refine your coding practices, such as writing clean, efficient code, using version control (e.g., Git), and documenting your work. These practices are essential for professional software development and will set you apart from other programmers.

The Key Elements of a Large Python Project

To succeed in a larger project, you must understand how to manage its various components. This involves a balance of planning, organization, and execution. Here are the key elements that should be considered when working on a large Python project:

Project Planning: Before writing a single line of code, it is crucial to plan your project. Define the problem, identify the requirements, and create a roadmap for how you'll tackle it. Think about the core features you want to implement, how you'll organize your code, and which tools you'll need.

- *Scope Definition*: What exactly does the project need to accomplish?

- *Requirements Gathering*: What inputs and outputs are needed?
- *Milestones*: Break the project into smaller, manageable phases. Set deadlines for each stage to ensure steady progress.

Design: Once you have a clear understanding of the project's scope, it's time to design the application. You can start with high-level designs and then move to more detailed designs. Consider the following:

- *Data Flow*: How will information be input, processed, and output?
- *Architecture*: Will the project be a command-line tool, a web application, or a desktop program? What technologies or libraries will you need to integrate with Python?
- *User Interface*: Will there be a graphical user interface (GUI), or will the project be text-based?

Breaking Down Tasks: Large projects can be overwhelming if you try to tackle everything at once. Break the project into manageable tasks or modules, and focus on completing one part at a time.

- *Functionality*: Focus on implementing one feature at a time, starting with the most essential ones.
- *Testing*: Write tests for each piece of functionality as you go. This ensures your code works correctly and minimizes bugs later on.

Iteration and Refinement: The first version of your project will not be perfect, and that's okay. It's essential to refine and iterate as you go. You'll likely find bugs, limitations, and inefficiencies during development, but don't be discouraged. Use feedback and testing to improve your code and design.

Documentation: Document your code and project to ensure others (or even yourself in the future) can understand and maintain it. Write clear comments within the code, create a README file to explain how to run the project, and include any installation or dependency instructions.

Version Control: Use version control tools like Git to track changes in your code, manage multiple versions, and collaborate with others. This is especially important when working on large projects to avoid code loss and ensure proper management of different stages of the project.

Testing: As you progress, write unit tests to verify that each part of your project functions correctly. Testing ensures that bugs are caught early, and changes to the code do not break existing functionality. Learn how to automate your testing process to make this step more efficient.

Final Deployment: After completing the coding, testing, and refinement stages, it's time to deploy the project. Whether you're uploading it to GitHub, deploying it to a web server, or creating an executable for a desktop application, deployment makes your project accessible to others. Be sure to follow the necessary steps to make it easy for others to install or use.

The Role of Collaboration in Large Projects

While you may be working solo on your learning journey, real-world projects often involve collaboration with others. Being able to collaborate on large projects is an invaluable skill in software development. Here are some strategies for effective collaboration:

- **Use Version Control**: Git and GitHub are indispensable tools for team collaboration. They allow multiple developers to work on the same project without stepping on each other's toes. Using branches for new features or bug fixes ensures that the main codebase stays clean.
- **Code Reviews**: Sharing your code with others for review helps spot bugs, improve design, and ensure adherence to best practices. Code reviews are a fundamental part of the software development process.
- **Agile Methodology**: Many large projects follow agile development practices, where development is broken down into short cycles, known

as sprints. Each sprint focuses on delivering a specific feature or solving a specific problem.
- **Communication**: Maintain clear communication with your collaborators. Use tools like Slack, email, or project management systems to stay connected and keep track of your progress.

Types of Real-World Projects You Can Build

As a beginner Python developer, it's essential to start with projects that are challenging but not overwhelming. Here are some project ideas to help you build real-world applications:

1. **Command-Line Tools**: Start by building practical command-line tools that automate tasks like file management, data analysis, or system monitoring.
2. **Web Scraping Applications**: Use libraries like requests and BeautifulSoup to build projects that scrape data from websites and process it for further use.
3. **Web Applications**: Using frameworks like Flask or Django, you can build fully functional web applications. This will introduce you to the concepts of web development, databases, and user authentication.
4. **Games**: Build simple text-based games or graphical games using libraries like Pygame. This will teach you about logic, handling user input, and rendering graphics.
5. **Data Analysis and Visualization**: Work with libraries like pandas, NumPy, and Matplotlib to process large datasets, analyze trends, and present the results in an insightful manner.
6. **Machine Learning**: Once you're comfortable with basic programming, you can explore machine learning projects using libraries like TensorFlow or Scikit-learn. Start by building models to predict outcomes based on data.

Large projects are an excellent way to reinforce your Python knowledge and apply your skills in real-world scenarios. By taking on these larger challenges, you will gain confidence in your ability to write code, solve complex problems, and build practical applications. The experience of working on bigger projects will not only help you improve your technical abilities but also prepare you for the demands of a professional software developer career.

In the following sections, we will explore several project ideas that will allow you to put everything you've learned into practice. Each project will require you to combine your understanding of Python and apply it creatively to solve problems. These projects are designed to be both fun and educational, providing you with the skills you need to continue building more advanced applications in the future.

Project 1: Text-Based Adventure Game

Integrating Conditionals, Loops, Functions, and String Manipulation

A text-based adventure game is an excellent way to apply a combination of basic Python concepts, including control flow (if-else statements, loops), functions, and string manipulation. In this project, you'll create a simple interactive game where the player navigates through different rooms, makes choices, and encounters challenges based on the input they provide.

Project Overview

The player starts in a room with several possible exits. As the player makes choices, the game responds with different scenarios and outcomes. The goal is to successfully navigate through the game by making the right decisions and avoiding traps. This type of project requires you to work with:

- **Conditionals** to determine how the game responds to player choices.
- **Loops** to allow the player to repeat actions until they reach a valid outcome.
- **Functions** to organize the game's logic and make the code more

modular and readable.
- **String Manipulation** to handle user input, create text-based descriptions, and display the narrative.

Key Concepts Covered:

- **Control Flow (Conditionals and Loops):** The game will rely on if-else statements and loops to manage player input and guide the game's progression.
- **Functions:** You'll define functions for major game components such as displaying a room description, getting the player's choice, and handling game outcomes.
- **String Manipulation:** Manipulating text, such as displaying different messages based on player input, creating dialogue options, and validating input.
- **Recursion (Optional):** If you want to add a bit more complexity, you can introduce recursion by allowing the game to restart from a checkpoint based on certain conditions.

Step-by-Step Guide to Building the Game
Initial Setup

Start by designing the basic structure of your game. Define a series of rooms that the player can visit, and set up a basic loop where the player can make choices and progress through different scenarios.

Here's how you can start:

```python
def start_game():
    print("Welcome to the Adventure Game!")
    print("You are in a dark room with two doors.")
    first_choice()

def first_choice():
```

```python
print("Do you go through the left door or the right door?")
choice = input("Enter 'left' or 'right': ").lower()

if choice == 'left':
    print("You find yourself in a treasure room!")
    treasure_room()
elif choice == 'right':
    print("You fall into a pit!")
    pit_room()
else:
    print("Invalid choice, try again.")
    first_choice()
```

Defining Rooms and Choices

Next, create more rooms and possible outcomes based on the player's decisions. Each room will have its own function, and you'll pass the player's choices through conditionals to determine which room or event they reach.

python

```
def treasure_room():
    print("Congratulations! You've found the treasure.")
    print("You have a choice to take the treasure or leave.")
    choice = input("Do you want to take the treasure? (yes/no): ").lower()

    if choice == 'yes':
        print("You take the treasure and become rich!")
        game_over()
    elif choice == 'no':
        print("You decide not to take the treasure and leave.")
        first_choice()
    else:
        print("Invalid choice, try again.")
        treasure_room()

def pit_room():
    print("You fall into a pit and are trapped!")
```

```python
    print("Do you want to try again or give up?")
    choice = input("Enter 'try' to attempt an
 escape or 'give up' to quit: ").lower()

    if choice == 'try':
        print("You manage to climb out of the pit!")
        first_choice()
    elif choice == 'give up':
        print("You gave up. Game over!")
        game_over()
    else:
        print("Invalid choice, try again.")
        pit_room()

def game_over():
    print("Game Over! Would you like to play again? (yes/no)")
    choice = input().lower()

    if choice == 'yes':
        start_game()
    elif choice == 'no':
        print("Thanks for playing!")
    else:
        print("Invalid input, try again.")
        game_over()
```

Function Breakdown and Game Flow

The game logic is broken down into smaller functions:

- start_game() initializes the game and prompts the player for their first choice.
- first_choice() handles the decision between two doors.
- treasure_room() and pit_room() define the different outcomes based on the player's decision after entering each room.
- game_over() gives the player the option to start over or quit.

This modular approach helps keep the code clean and manageable, especially when the game expands.

Adding String Manipulation for Dynamic Text

To make the game more dynamic, you can add user names, random events, or more descriptive text. For instance, you can greet the player with their name, or give them the option to choose their character's name at the start of the game.

```python
def start_game():
    print("Welcome to the Adventure Game!")
    name = input("What is your name, adventurer? ")
    print(f"Hello, {name}! You are in a dark room with two doors.")
    first_choice(name)

def first_choice(name):
    print(f"{name}, do you go through the left door or the right door?")
    choice = input("Enter 'left' or 'right': ").lower()

    if choice == 'left':
        print(f"{name}, you find yourself in a treasure room!")
        treasure_room(name)
    elif choice == 'right':
        print(f"{name}, you fall into a pit!")
        pit_room(name)
    else:
        print("Invalid choice, try again.")
        first_choice(name)
```

Here, the player's name is used to personalize the experience and make the game more engaging.

Adding Loops and Recursion

Notice how we use loops in conjunction with conditionals to ensure that the player's choices are valid and to let them retry if they enter an invalid input. You can also use recursion for replaying the game or retrying a section, as shown in game_over() and first_choice() functions.

Further Enhancements

To make your game more complex and interesting, consider adding:

- **Inventory System:** Allow the player to collect items and use them later in the game.
- **Multiple Rooms and Paths:** Create more rooms and non-linear pathways that allow for different storylines and challenges.
- **Combat System:** Introduce basic combat with enemies using random numbers to simulate attacks and damage.
- **Timer/Countdown:** Add a time element that challenges the player to make decisions quickly or face consequences.

Example of an Expanded Game

Here's a brief expansion of the game, adding a simple inventory system:

python

```
def start_game():
    inventory = []  # Initialize player's inventory
    print("Welcome to the Adventure Game!")
    print("You are in a dark room with two doors.")
    first_choice(inventory)

def first_choice(inventory):
    print("Do you go through the left door or the right door?")
    choice = input("Enter 'left' or 'right': ").lower()

    if choice == 'left':
        print("You find a shiny sword!")
        inventory.append("sword")
        treasure_room(inventory)
    elif choice == 'right':
        print("You fall into a pit!")
        pit_room(inventory)
    else:
        print("Invalid choice, try again.")
```

PUTTING IT ALL TOGETHER – PROJECTS AND REAL-WORLD...

```
    first_choice(inventory)

def treasure_room(inventory):
    print("You are in the treasure room!")
    if "sword" in inventory:
        print("With your sword, you feel confident!")
    else:
        print("You don't have a weapon, be careful!")
    # Continue the game...
```

Now, when the player finds the sword, it is added to their inventory, and later decisions are influenced by whether or not they possess it.

Creating a text-based adventure game like this is an engaging and fun way to practice a wide range of Python concepts. As you work through this project, you'll improve your understanding of conditionals, loops, functions, and string manipulation. You'll also gain valuable experience in organizing code and structuring larger programs.

This project serves as a solid foundation for building more complex games and applications in Python. You can always expand the game by adding new features, more rooms, and branching paths to enhance the player's experience.

Project 2: Expense Tracker
File Handling, Data Structures, Basic OOP

An **Expense Tracker** is a simple yet powerful application that allows users to manage and track their spending. The goal of this project is to integrate file handling, data structures (like lists and dictionaries), and basic object-oriented programming (OOP) to store, retrieve, and manipulate data efficiently.

In this project, you'll:

- Use **file handling** to store and retrieve user data (expenses, categories, dates).

- Use **data structures** (lists and dictionaries) to manage and organize expenses.
- Utilize **basic OOP** to model the structure of the program, such as creating classes for managing expenses and users.

By building this project, you will understand how to:

- Structure programs with classes and functions for better organization and modularity.
- Handle persistent data through file operations.
- Use lists, dictionaries, and other data structures to store and process user information efficiently.

Project Overview

The Expense Tracker will have a user interface (CLI) where the user can:

1. **Add expenses**: Store an expense along with its category, amount, and date.
2. **View expenses**: Display a list of expenses.
3. **View expenses by category**: Filter and show expenses by category.
4. **Save data to a file**: Persist all the user's data, so they can continue tracking expenses after closing the program.
5. **View total spending**: Calculate the total amount spent.

The application will consist of the following:

- **Class for Expense**: A class to define and manage the expenses.
- **Class for Expense Tracker**: A class to handle operations like adding, viewing, and saving expenses.
- **File Handling**: To save and load expenses to and from a CSV file.

Key Concepts Covered:

- **File Handling**: Reading from and writing to files.
- **OOP (Classes and Objects)**: Managing expenses using classes to encapsulate data and behavior.
- **Data Structures**: Using dictionaries and lists to manage multiple expenses and categories.
- **Basic Arithmetic and Logic**: Calculating the total of expenses, filtering by category.

Step-by-Step Guide to Building the Expense Tracker

Define the Expense Class The Expense class will encapsulate information about an individual expense, such as the name, category, amount, and date.

```python
class Expense:
    def __init__(self, name, category, amount, date):
        self.name = name
        self.category = category
        self.amount = amount
        self.date = date

    def __str__(self):
        return f"{self.name} ({self.category}) - ${self.amount} on {self.date}"
```

In the Expense class:

- __init__() initializes the object with values for name, category, amount, and date.
- __str__() provides a formatted string representation of the expense, which is useful for displaying in the UI.

Define the ExpenseTracker Class The ExpenseTracker class will manage all expenses. It will allow adding expenses, viewing expenses, and saving/loading from a file.

```python
class ExpenseTracker:
    def __init__(self):
        self.expenses = []

    def add_expense(self, name, category, amount, date):
        expense = Expense(name, category, amount, date)
        self.expenses.append(expense)

    def view_expenses(self):
        if not self.expenses:
            print("No expenses recorded.")
            return
        for expense in self.expenses:
            print(expense)

    def view_expenses_by_category(self, category):
        filtered_expenses = [exp for exp in self.expenses if exp.category.lower() == category.lower()]
        if not filtered_expenses:
            print(f"No expenses found for the category '{category}'.")
            return
        for expense in filtered_expenses:
            print(expense)

    def total_spending(self):
        return sum(expense.amount for expense in self.expenses)

    def save_to_file(self, filename):
        with open(filename, 'w') as file:
            for expense in self.expenses:
                file.write(f"{expense.name},{expense.category},{expense.amount},{expense.date}\n")

    def load_from_file(self, filename):
```

```python
        try:
            with open(filename, 'r') as file:
                for line in file:
                    name, category, amount, date =
                    line.strip().split(',')
                    self.add_expense(name,
 category, float(amount), date)
        except FileNotFoundError:
            print("No saved expenses found. Starting fresh.")
```

In the ExpenseTracker class:

- add_expense() creates an Expense object and adds it to the list of expenses.
- view_expenses() prints all the expenses stored.
- view_expenses_by_category() filters and displays expenses by a given category.
- total_spending() calculates the total amount of money spent.
- save_to_file() saves all expenses to a file in CSV format.
- load_from_file() loads expenses from a CSV file.

Main Program and User Interface The program will provide the user with a command-line interface to interact with the tracker. The user can choose to add expenses, view expenses, or exit the program.

```python
python

def main():
    tracker = ExpenseTracker()
    tracker.load_from_file("expenses.csv")
    print("Welcome to the Expense Tracker!")

    while True:
        print("\n1. Add an expense")
        print("2. View all expenses")
```

```
        print("3. View expenses by category")
        print("4. View total spending")
        print("5. Exit")
        choice = input("Please choose an option (1-5): ")

        if choice == '1':
            name = input("Enter the expense name: ")
            category = input("Enter the category: ")
            amount = float(input("Enter the amount: "))
            date = input("Enter the date (YYYY-MM-DD): ")
            tracker.add_expense(name, category, amount, date)
            print("Expense added.")
        elif choice == '2':
            tracker.view_expenses()
        elif choice == '3':
            category = input("Enter category to filter by: ")
            tracker.view_expenses_by_category(category)
        elif choice == '4':
            print(f"Total spending: ${tracker
.total_spending():.2f}")
        elif choice == '5':
            tracker.save_to_file("expenses.csv")
            print("Expenses saved. Goodbye!")
            break
        else:
            print("Invalid choice, please try again.")
```

In the main() function:

- The program loads any existing expenses from the expenses.csv file using load_from_file().
- It displays a menu and asks the user for their input. Depending on the choice, it calls the relevant methods to add, view, or save expenses.
- The program saves all expenses to the expenses.csv file when the user exits.

Running the Expense Tracker To run the Expense Tracker, simply call the main() function:

```python
if __name__ == "__main__":
    main()
```

When running the program, you can:

- Add expenses by providing details like the name, category, amount, and date.
- View all expenses or filter by category.
- Check the total amount spent.
- Exit the program, which will save your data to a file for later use.

Example Session:

```markdown
Welcome to the Expense Tracker!

1. Add an expence
2. View all expenses
3. View expenses by category
4. View total spending
5. Exit
Please choose an option (1-5): 1
Enter the expense name: Coffee
Enter the category: Food
Enter the amount: 3.50
Enter the date (YYYY-MM-DD): 2024-11-01
Expense added.

1. Add an expense
2. View all expenses
3. View expenses by category
4. View total spending
```

```
5. Exit
Please choose an option (1-5): 2
Coffee (Food) - $3.50 on 2024-11-01

1. Add an expense
2. View all expenses
3. View expenses by category
4. View total spending
5. Exit
Please choose an option (1-5): 4
Total spending: $3.50
```

Further Enhancements

To enhance the Expense Tracker, you can add:

- **Categorized Reports**: Generate reports for each category and show total spending per category.
- **Budgeting**: Allow users to set a budget and compare their spending against it.
- **Multiple Users**: Extend the program to handle multiple users by adding a User class and storing each user's expenses separately.

Building an Expense Tracker is a practical way to integrate file handling, data structures, and basic OOP. By structuring the program with classes, functions, and handling data persistently, you gain a solid foundation for building more complex applications. This project also serves as an excellent example of how to structure real-world applications that manage user data and perform persistent operations like saving and loading.

Project 3: Basic Calculator with History
Lists, Functions, File I/O

A **Basic Calculator with History** is a great project to solidify your understanding of functions, lists, and file input/output (I/O) in Python. This project allows users to perform basic arithmetic operations (addition, subtraction, multiplication, and division) and stores the history of operations performed. You will be able to recall previously performed calculations, making it a useful tool for learning Python while developing practical skills.

This project integrates:

- **Lists** to store the history of calculations.
- **Functions** to organize operations like addition, subtraction, multiplication, and division.
- **File I/O** to save and load the calculation history so that users can access their previous results even after restarting the program.

By completing this project, you'll learn how to:

- Manage and manipulate a history of operations using Python lists.
- Implement arithmetic operations using functions.
- Use file handling to store and retrieve user data, creating a persistent calculator experience.

Project Overview

The **Basic Calculator with History** will have a user interface (CLI) where the user can:

1. Perform arithmetic operations (addition, subtraction, multiplication, division).
2. View the history of previous calculations.
3. Save the history to a file for future use.
4. Load the history from the file when the program starts.

The program will consist of the following components:

- **Calculator Functions**: Functions for performing basic operations like addition, subtraction, multiplication, and division.

- **History Management**: A system for storing, displaying, and saving the history of operations.
- **File Handling**: Saving and loading the history from a text file.
- **Menu**: A simple CLI that allows users to interact with the program.

Step-by-Step Guide to Building the Basic Calculator with History

Define Calculator Functions The first step is to create functions for the basic arithmetic operations: addition, subtraction, multiplication, and division.

```python
def add(x, y):
    return x + y

def subtract(x, y):
    return x - y

def multiply(x, y):
    return x * y

def divide(x, y):
    if y == 0:
        return "Error! Division by zero."
    return x / y
```

- Each function takes two arguments (x and y) and returns the result of the operation.
- The divide() function includes a check for division by zero to avoid errors.

Manage Calculation History We'll store the calculation history in a list. Each time the user performs a calculation, the result will be appended to the list. We'll also implement functions to display and save this history.

```python
history = []

def add_to_history(operation, result):
    history.append(f"{operation} = {result}")

def view_history():
    if not history:
        print("No history available.")
        return
    for record in history:
        print(record)

def save_history(filename):
    with open(filename, 'w') as file:
        for record in history:
            file.write(f"{record}\n")
    print("History saved to file.")

def load_history(filename):
    try:
        with open(filename, 'r') as file:
            for line in file:
                history.append(line.strip())
        print("History loaded from file.")
    except FileNotFoundError:
        print("No previous history found. Starting fresh.")
```

In the history list:

- add_to_history() appends each operation and its result as a string.
- view_history() prints all the history records.
- save_history() saves the history to a text file, making it persistent across sessions.
- load_history() loads the history from a file when the program starts.

Build the Main Program and User Interface Now, we create the main program, which will allow the user to interact with the calculator. The program will prompt the user to choose an operation and will call the appropriate function based on the choice.

python

```
def main():
    load_history("history.txt")

    while True:
        print("\nCalculator Menu:")
        print("1. Add")
        print("2. Subtract")
        print("3. Multiply")
        print("4. Divide")
        print("5. View History")
        print("6. Save History")
        print("7. Exit")

        choice = input("Choose an option (1-7): ")

        if choice == '1':
            x = float(input("Enter first number: "))
            y = float(input("Enter second number: "))
            result = add(x, y)
            print(f"Result: {result}")
            add_to_history(f"{x} + {y}", result)
        elif choice == '2':
            x = float(input("Enter first number: "))
            y = float(input("Enter second number: "))
            result = subtract(x, y)
            print(f"Result: {result}")
            add_to_history(f"{x} - {y}", result)
        elif choice == '3':
            x = float(input("Enter first number: "))
            y = float(input("Enter second number: "))
            result = multiply(x, y)
            print(f"Result: {result}")
            add_to_history(f"{x} * {y}", result)
```

```python
        elif choice == '4':
            x = float(input("Enter first number: "))
            y = float(input("Enter second number: "))
            result = divide(x, y)
            print(f"Result: {result}")
            add_to_history(f"{x} / {y}", result)
        elif choice == '5':
            view_history()
        elif choice == '6':
            save_history("history.txt")
        elif choice == '7':
            print("Exiting program.")
            save_history("history.txt")
            break
        else:
            print("Invalid choice, please try again.")
```

In the main() function:

- The program loads the history from the history.txt file using load_history().
- It displays a menu and prompts the user to choose an operation.
- Based on the user's choice, the program performs the respective arithmetic operation and updates the history.
- The program provides options to view the history, save it, or exit.
- When the user exits, the history is saved to the file to preserve it for the next session.

Running the Basic Calculator To run the program, call the main() function:

python

```
if __name__ == "__main__":
    main()
```

When running the program, you can:

- Perform basic arithmetic operations.
- View the history of previous calculations.
- Save and load the history to/from a text file.

Example Session:

```markdown
Calculator Menu:
1. Add
2. Subtract
3. Multiply
4. Divide
5. View History
6. Save History
7. Exit
Choose an option (1-7): 1
Enter first number: 5
Enter second number: 3
Result: 8.0

Calculator Menu:
1. Add
2. Subtract
3. Multiply
4. Divide
5. View History
6. Save History
7. Exit
Choose an option (1-7): 5
5 + 3 = 8.0

Calculator Menu:
1. Add
2. Subtract
3. Multiply
4. Divide
5. View History
6. Save History
```

```
7. Exit
Choose an option (1-7): 6
History saved to file.

Calculator Menu:
1. Add
2. Subtract
3. Multiply
4. Divide
5. View History
6. Save History
7. Exit
Choose an option (1-7): 7
Exiting program.
History saved to file.
```

Further Enhancements

To enhance the **Basic Calculator with History**, you could add:

- **Multiple Users**: Allow different users to have their own history and settings.
- **Advanced Operations**: Implement more complex operations such as exponentiation, square roots, or trigonometric functions.
- **Graphical User Interface (GUI)**: Convert the program to a graphical interface using libraries like Tkinter or PyQt.

The **Basic Calculator with History** project is a great way to learn about functions, lists, and file handling in Python. By building this simple calculator, you will practice writing modular code, handling persistent data, and creating a user-friendly CLI. This project is a stepping stone toward more complex applications, and its flexibility makes it easy to expand and modify according to your learning needs.

Project 4: Password Strength Checker
String Processing, Regular Expressions, File Handling

A **Password Strength Checker** is an essential tool that can evaluate the strength of a password based on predefined criteria. It can be implemented using string processing, regular expressions, and file handling to allow users to test and store passwords. This project helps you practice working with strings, regular expressions for pattern matching, and file I/O operations in Python.

This project will:

- Use **String Processing** to evaluate passwords.
- Leverage **Regular Expressions** to validate password patterns (such as checking for uppercase, lowercase, numbers, and special characters).
- Utilize **File Handling** to store valid passwords and their corresponding strength categories (e.g., weak, medium, strong).

By the end of this project, you'll be able to:

- Create a robust password strength evaluation system using Python.
- Use regular expressions to check password complexity.
- Process strings efficiently and handle file I/O operations for saving results.

Project Overview

The **Password Strength Checker** will:
Prompt the user to input a password.
Evaluate the strength of the password based on:

- Length: The password must be at least 8 characters long.
- Character variety: The password must include uppercase letters, lowercase letters, numbers, and special characters.

Categorize the password as **Weak**, **Medium**, or **Strong** based on the evaluation criteria.
Save the password and its strength category to a file for record-keeping.

PUTTING IT ALL TOGETHER – PROJECTS AND REAL-WORLD...

The program will be structured as follows:

- **Password Evaluation Function**: A function that checks the password strength based on the criteria.
- **Regular Expression Patterns**: Patterns to match and verify required characters in the password.
- **File Handling**: A system to save and load passwords and their strength categories.

Step-by-Step Guide to Building the Password Strength Checker

Define Regular Expressions for Password Validation We'll use regular expressions to validate the presence of different types of characters in the password (uppercase, lowercase, digits, and special characters). The regular expression module re in Python is perfect for this task.

```python
import re

def is_strong_password(password):
    # Check password length
    if len(password) < 8:
        return False
    # Check if password contains at least one lowercase letter
    if not re.search(r"[a-z]", password):
        return False
    # Check if password contains at least one uppercase letter
    if not re.search(r"[A-Z]", password):
        return False
    # Check if password contains at least one number
    if not re.search(r"\d", password):
        return False
    # Check if password contains at least one special character
    if not re.search
(r"[@$!%*?&]", password):
        return False
```

```
return True
```

- The is_strong_password() function checks if the password is at least 8 characters long and includes:
- At least one lowercase letter (r"[a-z]").
- At least one uppercase letter (r"[A-Z]").
- At least one digit (r"\d").
- At least one special character (r"[@$!%*?&]").
- If all conditions are met, the password is considered strong.

Categorize Passwords Based on Strength Now that we have a function to check whether a password is strong, we need a way to categorize passwords as **Weak, Medium,** or **Strong.**

```python
def categorize_password(password):
    if len(password) < 8:
        return "Weak"
    elif len(password) < 12:
        return "Medium"
    elif is_strong_password(password):
        return "Strong"
    return "Weak"
```

- Passwords that are shorter than 8 characters are categorized as "Weak".
- Passwords that are 8 to 12 characters long and pass basic checks are categorized as "Medium".
- Passwords that meet the strength criteria (length and character variety) are categorized as "Strong".

File Handling: Storing and Loading Passwords The program will store the evaluated passwords and their strength categories in a text file. This will allow users to keep a record of the passwords they've tested and see their strength ratings.

```python
def save_password_strength(password, strength,
filename="passwords.txt"):
    with open(filename, "a") as file:
        file.write(f"{password} - {strength}\n")
    print(f"Password and strength
'{strength}' saved to file.")

def load_saved_passwords
(filename="passwords.txt"):
    try:
        with open(filename, "r") as file:
            print("\nSaved Passwords and Strengths:")
            for line in file:
                print(line.strip())
    except FileNotFoundError:
        print("No saved passwords found.")
```

- save_password_strength() appends each password and its corresponding strength to a file (passwords.txt).
- load_saved_passwords() reads the file and displays the list of saved passwords and their strength.

Build the User Interface We will now put everything together into a user interface where users can input passwords, check their strength, and save or load results.

```python
def main():
    while True:
        print("\nPassword Strength Checker")
```

```python
        print("1. Check Password Strength")
        print("2. View Saved Passwords")
        print("3. Exit")
        choice = input("Choose an option (1-3): ")

        if choice == '1':
            password = input("Enter password to check strength: ")
            strength = categorize_password(password)
            print(f"Password strength: {strength}")
            save_option = input("Do you want to save this password? (yes/no): ").strip().lower()
            if save_option == 'yes':
                save_password_strength(password, strength)
        elif choice == '2':
            load_saved_passwords()
        elif choice == '3':
            print("Exiting program.")
            break
        else:
            print("Invalid option. Please try again.")

if __name__ == "__main__":
    main()
```

- The main() function allows users to choose:
- Check a password's strength.
- View previously saved passwords and their strengths.
- Exit the program.
- When checking password strength, users can opt to save the result to a file.

Running the Program When the user runs the program, they will be able to check the strength of passwords and view previously tested ones.

Example Interaction:

```
sql
```

```
Password Strength Checker
1. Check Password Strength
2. View Saved Passwords
3. Exit
Choose an option (1-3): 1
Enter password to check strength: myP@ssw0rd123
Password strength: Strong
Do you want to save this password? (yes/no): yes
Password and strength 'Strong' saved to file.

Password Strength Checker
1. Check Password Strength
2. View Saved Passwords
3. Exit
Choose an option (1-3): 2
Saved Passwords and Strengths:
myP@ssw0rd123 - Strong
```

Further Enhancements

You can expand the **Password Strength Checker** by:

- Adding more detailed password complexity checks (e.g., checking for consecutive characters or dictionary words).
- Incorporating a graphical user interface (GUI) using Tkinter for better usability.
- Creating a password strength report with suggestions to improve weak passwords.
- Implementing a password generator that creates random strong passwords based on specified criteria.

The **Password Strength Checker** is a valuable project for anyone learning Python, as it incorporates string processing, regular expressions, and file handling. By building this tool, you will improve your understanding of pattern matching with regular expressions and strengthen your skills in managing data using files. This project also provides a practical application, as it can be used to help users maintain secure passwords.

Project 5: Personal Task Manager
Using OOP Concepts, Dictionaries, File Handling

This **Personal Task Manager** project is designed to enable users to manage their daily tasks effectively by creating, updating, and organizing their to-do lists. The manager will be built using **Object-Oriented Programming (OOP)** principles, **Dictionaries** for storing task data, and **File Handling** for persistent storage.

This project aims to practice and deepen your understanding of:
- Building classes and objects with defined attributes and methods.
- Using dictionaries to store multiple data points per task.
- Implementing file handling to save and retrieve tasks for ongoing use.

Upon completing this project, you'll have an interactive task management system that saves data across sessions, allowing users to effectively track and manage tasks over time.

Step-by-Step Guide to Building the Personal Task Manager
Step 1: Defining the Task Class

The Task class represents individual tasks, including essential attributes like task name, description, due date, and status. This class should also provide methods for marking a task as completed and displaying task details.

PUTTING IT ALL TOGETHER – PROJECTS AND REAL-WORLD...

```python

class Task:
    def __init__(self, name, description, due_date,
    status="Pending"):
        self.name = name
        self.description = description
        self.due_date = due_date
        self.status = status

    def __str__(self):
        return f"Task: {self.name}\nDescription:
    {self.description}\nDue Date:
 {self.due_date}\
nStatus: {self.status}"

    def mark_completed(self):
        self.status = "Completed"
```

Explanation:

- The __init__() method sets up task attributes.
- The __str__() method allows for a formatted printout of each task's details.
- The mark_completed() method updates the task's status to "Completed."

Step 2: Creating the TaskManager Class

The TaskManager class will manage multiple tasks, using a dictionary to store task instances by name. It includes methods to add, remove, update, view tasks, and manage file storage.

```python

class TaskManager:
    def __init__(self):
        self.tasks = {}
```

```python
    def add_task(self, task):
        self.tasks[task.name] = task

    def remove_task(self, task_name):
        if task_name in self.tasks:
            del self.tasks[task_name]
        else:
            print(f"Task '{task_name}' not found.")

    def view_tasks(self):
        if not self.tasks:
            print("No tasks available.")
        for task in self.tasks.values():
            print(task)
            print("-" * 40)

    def update_task_status(self, task_name):
        if task_name in self.tasks:
self.tasks[task_name].mark_completed()
print(f"Task '{task_name}'
 marked as completed.")
        else:
            print(f"Task '{task_name}' not found.")
```

Step 3: Adding File Handling for Persistence

The TaskManager class will now include methods to save tasks to a file and load them from a file to provide persistent storage.

python

```
    def save_tasks(self, filename="tasks.txt"):
        with open(filename, "w") as file:
for task in self.tasks.values():
file.write(f"{task.name},
{task.description},
{task.due_date},{task.status}\n")
        print("Tasks saved to file.")
```

```python
    def load_tasks(self, filename="tasks.txt"):
        try:
            with open(filename, "r") as file:
                for line in file:
                    name, description, due_date, status = line.strip().split(",")
                    task = Task(name, description, due_date, status)
                    self.add_task(task)
            print("Tasks loaded from file.")
        except FileNotFoundError:
            print("No saved tasks found.")
```

Building the User Interface

The main() function below serves as an interface for interacting with the Task Manager. Users can add tasks, view tasks, update their status, and save/load tasks from a file.

python

```
def main():
    task_manager = TaskManager()
    task_manager.load_tasks()  # Load tasks from the file if available

    while True:
        print("\nPersonal Task Manager")
        print("1. Add Task")
        print("2. View Tasks")
        print("3. Remove Task")
        print("4. Mark Task as Completed")
        print("5. Save Tasks")
        print("6. Exit")
        choice = input("Choose an option (1-6): ")

        if choice == '1':
```

```
            name = input("Enter task name: ")
            description = input("Enter task description: ")
            due_date = input("Enter due date (YYYY-MM-DD): ")
            task = Task(name, description, due_date)
            task_manager.add_task(task)
            print("Task added successfully.")
        elif choice == '2':
            task_manager.view_tasks()
        elif choice == '3':
            name = input("Enter task name to remove: ")
            task_manager.remove_task(name)
        elif choice == '4':
            name = input("Enter task name to mark as completed: ")
            task_manager.update_task_status(name)
        elif choice == '5':
            task_manager.save_tasks()
        elif choice == '6':
            print("Exiting program.")
            break
        else:
            print("Invalid option. Please try again.")

if __name__ == "__main__":
    main()
```

Key Project Insights

File Handling and Persistence:

The save and load functions ensure that tasks remain accessible after the program ends, simulating a real application's persistent storage.

Error Handling:

The load_tasks() method gracefully handles a FileNotFoundError if no saved tasks are available, ensuring a smooth user experience without unexpected crashes.

Encapsulation of Data with OOP:

The Task class encapsulates individual task data, while the TaskManager class handles higher-level functionality, adhering to OOP principles that improve maintainability.

User Interaction and Interface Design:
The menu-driven system allows users to perform essential task management functions with ease, providing a good example of a basic command-line interface (CLI).

Dictionaries for Quick Data Lookup:
By storing tasks in a dictionary, you ensure efficient lookup and removal by task name, demonstrating practical applications of data structures in project design.

Project Extension Ideas
This project is extensible and can be expanded with additional features such as:

- **Task Prioritization:** Allow users to assign priority levels (e.g., High, Medium, Low) and sort tasks by priority.
- **Task Reminders:** Implement a notification system that reminds users of approaching task deadlines.
- **Graphical Interface:** Integrate Tkinter to create a GUI version of the Personal Task Manager.
- **Export Options:** Enable exporting tasks to CSV or PDF formats for reporting purposes.
- **Data Analysis:** Incorporate a summary feature that provides insights, such as the number of tasks completed in a month.

The **Personal Task Manager** is a great way to deepen your understanding of object-oriented programming, dictionaries, and file handling. Through this project, you'll gain hands-on experience in structuring a multi-feature program that has real-world applications, all while reinforcing your knowledge of fundamental Python concepts.

Summary of Key Concepts and Skills Covered

The **Personal Task Manager** project combines foundational Python concepts with practical applications, creating a well-rounded experience for beginners. Here's a summary of the essential concepts and skills covered in this chapter:

1. **Object-Oriented Programming (OOP)**
- **Classes and Objects:**
- This project reinforced the understanding of classes (Task and TaskManager) to model real-world concepts, encapsulating data and behavior into logical units.
- **Attributes and Methods:**
- The use of attributes (such as name, description, due_date, and status) and methods (e.g., mark_completed() and __str__()) demonstrated how to define and work with class properties.
- **Encapsulation:**
- By keeping all task-related functionality within classes, the project encapsulated data, improving code organization and maintainability.

2. **Dictionaries for Data Storage**

- The dictionary structure enabled quick access, storage, and manipulation of tasks by name, showcasing the advantages of using dictionaries for structured, dynamic data.

3. **File Handling for Persistent Data**

- **Reading and Writing to Files:**
- Saving and loading tasks to and from a file introduced basic file handling (open(), write(), read(), etc.), simulating data persistence across sessions.

- **Error Handling:**
- The use of try-except for FileNotFoundError provided insights into handling potential errors gracefully, ensuring a smooth user experience.

4. **User Interface with Command-Line Interactions**

    - **Interactive CLI Design:**
    - The menu-driven interface used in main() allowed for intuitive interaction, reinforcing input handling and conditional operations (if-elif structure) in a command-line setting.
    - **User Prompting and Validation:**
    - By prompting users to select actions and enter task details, the project demonstrated how to build a responsive, user-friendly application.

5. **Practical Application of Python Basics**

    - **String Manipulation:**
    - Displaying task details and formatting outputs helped in understanding string manipulation.
    - **Looping through Data:**
    - The view_tasks() method provided practice in iterating over dictionary values, a common operation in Python programming.

Skill Reinforcement and Real-World Relevance

- **Combining Concepts into Real Projects:**
- This project brought together various programming fundamentals, giving you practical experience in combining multiple concepts into a cohesive, functioning application.
- **Project Extensibility:**
- The **Personal Task Manager** sets a foundation for further development. Adding features like task priority, GUI integration, or notifica-

tion reminders would enhance functionality, making the project more applicable to real-world needs.

By completing this project, you've gained experience with Python's core programming principles while building an interactive application that mirrors real-world task management tools. These skills and insights lay a strong foundation for tackling larger, more complex projects in Python.

www.ingramcontent.com/pod-product-compliance
Lightning Source LLC
Chambersburg PA
CBHW052138220526
45471CB00004B/1435